Information Distribution

Issues for the

90s

Information Distribution

Issues for the

90s

Edited by Betty Unruh
Wendy Schipper

The National Federation of
Abstracting and Information Services
Philadelphia, PA

The National Federation of Abstracting and Information Services
1429 Walnut Street, Philadelphia, PA 19102
© 1991 by The National Federation of Abstracting and Information Services
All rights reserved. Published 1991.

Printed in the United States of America.

ISBN 0-942308-30-1

Table of Contents

Acknowledgements

The authors of *Information Distribution Issues for the 90s* are owed special thanks for their clear-sighted assessments of the past, present, and future of information distribution. Well-written and broad in scope, each author's chapter stands on its own. Together, the chapters form a meaningful guide to tomorrow's distribution issues.

Kim Hayden and JoAnn Benussi at NFAIS Headquarters are applauded for their efforts organizing and formatting the text. This was Kim's initiation into the world of NFAIS publications; she was a trooper throughout the process. JoAnn put the final, beautifying touches to the book. Thanks are extended to Eileen Cleveland, as well, for designing and preparing the cover of *Distribution Issues*.

About the Authors

Since 1988, **Pauline Angione-Zoellick** has been an information consultant in product design and implementation services handling all phases of database development from market analysis to final design and testing. Previously, she was Product Manager at University Microfilms, International and Director, Software Products at the Institute for Scientific Information (ISI). From 1972 to 1979, Ms. Angione-Zoellick was an Assistant Professor of Library Science at the Rosary College Graduate School of Library Science. She has delivered numerous papers at information industry meetings including the American Library Association meeting, CD-ROM Expo, and the International Online Information Meeting. Ms. Angione-Zoellick has a BS in Pre-Med Biology/Chemistry from Nazareth College and a MA in Library and Information Science from the University of Chicago.

Dennis Auld is Director of PsycINFO, a database produced by the American Pschological Association (APA). He is renowned in the industry as the creator of ABI/INFORM, a database containing abstracts of business and management publications. Mr. Auld's career in the information industry began at Data Courier in 1974. He was promoted to Operations Vice President in 1977, Executive Vice President in 1980, and was named President in 1983. Mr. Auld is well versed in the history and development of the information industry, the technology of database publishing, and new product development. Aside from being a member of the American Society for Information Science (ASIS), the International Council for Scientific and Technical Information (ICSTI), and the Information Industry Association (IIA), he is Past-President of the Association of Information and Dissemination Centers (ASIDIC) and has been elected to serve on the 1991 NFAIS Board of Directors. Mr. Auld holds a BS in economics from the University of Oregon and a MBA from Portland State University.

Since 1985, **Bette Brunelle** has been the Director of New Product Development and Research and Development for BRS, responsible for research, design, and implementation of new products. In this capacity, she has led teams to develop the BRS link, medspell, plurals, and table-of-contents features; the BRS Order System; and the BRS/CD interface. From 1983-1985, Ms. Brunelle served as Director of Production at BRS, in charge of design, programming, and data entry for database services. She is also a member of the American Society for Information Science (ASIS). Ms. Brunelle received a BS in psychology from Johns Hopkins University and a MLS from SUNY Albany.

Prior to relocating to California, **Caroline Hall** was Manager of Database Services at PsycINFO. In that position, she was responsible for negotiating contracts for electronic and CD-ROM products and planning budgets for the marketing and administrative divisions of PsycINFO. Previously, Ms. Hall was Marketing Coordinator at Rhodeside & Harwell, Incorporated, where she developed marketing leads, wrote and produced proposals, and coordinated production of planning reports. From 1985 to 1987, Ms. Hall was an Information Specialist at Towers, Perrin, Forster & Crosby. She majored in english at the California State Polytechnic University and studied medical technology at Oregon State University.

Bonnie Lawlor is currently Executive Vice President of the Database Publishing Division at the Institute for Scientific Information (ISI). She began her career in chemical information in 1967 as an indexer for ISI where she has continued her professional growth for the past 22 years. Ms. Lawlor is active in the American Chemical Society (ACS), currently as Chair of the ACS Division of Chemical Information. She is also Past President of NFAIS and on the Board of Directors of the Pennsylvania Library Network (PALINET). She has a BS in chemistry from St. Joseph's University and a MBA from the Wharton School of the University of Pennsylvania.

Foreword

The dynamic nature of information and the kaleidoscopic shapes it assumes make it a fascinating subject to explore. Distinguishing the implications of new distribution channels, media, markets, and technology in the 90s is no easy task, yet the authors of *Information Distribution Issues for the 90s*--Pauline Angione-Zoellick, Dennis Auld, Bette Brunelle, Caroline Hall, and Bonnie Lawlor--have gallantly taken the plunge. Drawing upon a depth of industry expertise, they project a proactive, rather than reactive, approach to the issues raised by new distribution modes.

New media, markets, and information content have propelled information products and services into unexplored territory. Product development in the 90s has and will continue to advance to new technological frontiers; it will also be driven by a new market of end users. Database producers will be redefined as database publishers. The lines between publishers and vendors will blur as publishers become more involved in creating, packaging, and delivering data. A supply side orientation will be replaced by a demand side approach on the part of database publishers as they deal with the duality of information as both a product and service. Market needs will motivate future directions in the database business.

Innovation in the 90s is expected in the areas of electronic (full text) publishing; gateways; university consortia; customized and real time online databases; natural language interfaces; gigabit transmission and storage; multimedia applications; improved, faster, and "larger" CD-ROMs; fiber optic networks; and expert systems. What issues are at the heart of these developments? Pricing; marketing; primary publisher relationships; leases and licenses; and copyright issues.

Software and hardware solutions will proliferate in the 90s. Publishers will be faced with important decision-making options in the technical arena. Regarding software, the answers will lie in its potential for data enhancement, its compatibility with hardware, its general flexibility, and the publisher's internal production requirements. Scanning is the hot technology of the 90s. Publishers must weigh the advantages and disadvantages of optical character recognition (OCR) technology carefully. Standards--data preparation and CD-ROM--are raising both the publishers' and the market's consciousness in the 90s. Adherence to a standard will be an increasingly pressing decision.

Networks in the 90s are large-scale developments. National initiatives have been set in motion to establish high speed, high capacity information highways. Secondary services must be galvanized to take an active role in this ongoing movement. The demand for networked service, on the local level, is escalating rapidly. Network user communities are on the rise. Dial access networks, local area networks (LANs), and wide area networks (WANs) invite networked access to data. The issues raised by an expanded universe of information access as implied by networks are critical. They include property rights, pricing, licensing, and standards.

The emergence of new distribution vehicles spells change and adjustment for database publishers. The trend toward localized information resources is gaining steam. The 90s represent a time of reevaluation for database publishers. Pricing (of all media), marketing; customer and technical support; and licensing/networking agreements will have to be modified and adapted to fit the requirements of the 90s. The industry kaleidoscope will shift its information pieces around once again to make way for the 21st century.

1

The Product

To meet the challenges of information product development in the 90s, information publishers must first make certain cultural adjustments. They must evolve from being database producers to becoming database publishers; deal with the duality of information publishing as both a product and a service; recognize that they are in the middle of a "push-pull" marketplace; and tailor their production systems to meet end user needs. Once appropriately oriented, publishers may then begin to determine the database content, the distribution media, the distribution channels, and the user interface most appropriate for the end user--all in the context of external factors such as marketplace needs, primary publisher relationships, leases and licenses, and copyright issues.

The Value of Information

In his 1948 address to the New York State Publishers Association, Arthur Hays Sulzberger, then President of the *New York Times*, stated:

> "Obviously, a man's judgment cannot be better than the information on which he has based it. Give him the truth and he may still go wrong when he has the chance to be right, but give him no news or present him only with distorted and incomplete data, with ignorant, sloppy or biased reporting, with propaganda and deliberate falsehoods, and you destroy his whole reasoning process, and make him something less than a man."[1]

In the movie, Short Circuit, Number Five needed input (i.e., information) to survive.

In his 1989 novel, *The Negotiator*, Frederick Forsyth stresses the necessity of storing "a vast compendium of information about the oil industry and other industries, commercial needs, national economic performance, market trends, scientific advances, and people" for "to know what was going on and, more important, what was going to happen gave a man more power than political office or even money."[2]

The importance, or "value," of information is recognized in each of the above examples. Decisions result from information; but, just as the man described by Sulzberger cannot make valid judgments based on misinformation, Number Five malfunctioned because of his inability to assimilate the data he had ingested, and Cyrus Miller in Forsyth's novel failed because the information he received was often inaccurate and not timely. The information seekers of the 90s will be in a position wherein their very survival will depend on the content, quality, and timeliness of the information they receive. Solving this dilemma, then, becomes the challenge of the database publisher in the 90s.

This chapter is about the information product--its description and evolution--and where its future lies.

Cultural Adjustments

From Producer to Publisher

The first step in positioning a product that solves the information needs of the 90s is the database producer's evolution to the role of database publisher.

During the 80s, the term "producer" became the most used term chiefly because of the dominance of online vendors. Database publishers moved from a print orientation to an electronic orientation and became the producers of databases for online vendors' distribution. Virtually every field and major subject heading became available electronically; there was a tremendous outgrowth of databases.

From the vendors' standpoint, a consistent format for delivery of bibliographic information became essential to ensure interactive, electronic access to the disparate databases. To succeed, therefore, the online vendors became the major proponents for standards. Although the enforcement of standards concerned database publishers, compliance was mandatory if a publisher desired an outlet for its database. The result of standardization, regardless of the identity of the instigator, has been financially beneficial, in the long term, to both the online vendors and the database publishers. With the advent of CD-ROM, the producer-vendor relationship changed. Database publishers were no longer dependent upon online vendors for electronic distribution of their databases.

Although early CD-ROM applications appeared to mirror their online counterparts, the CD-ROMs contained diverse interfaces--a departure from the standardized mold cast by the online vendors. By evolving from the position of producer to database publisher, destiny is more within reach in the 90s.

Information as Both a Product and a Service

In this chapter, information will be addressed as a product; however, it is important to keep in mind that it bears the dual description of product and service. This duality is the single, most important factor affecting the marketability of information--the ease of producing a product versus the complexity of offering a service. Meeting the demands of this duality becomes a central issue in the 90s.

The "Push-Pull" Marketplace

The publisher's next move, in delivering a successful product, is to migrate from the supply side to the demand side of the marketing equation. This step requires not only database production in the traditional sense but also market research and end user investigation.

The first decade of electronic publishing was characterized by a replication of print products online and, later, on CD-ROM. Little difference existed between the appearance of an electronic record and its print equivalent, and the only advantages were the obvious--the efficiencies of use, the greater number of access points, and the increased timeliness of the material presented. Early electronic applications targeted well-defined market segments in business, education, and library markets.

Morris Goldstein, President of Information Access Company (IAC), in a presentation at the 1990 NFAIS Annual Conference, described the 80s as a decade of market segmentation--a market that, underneath its surface homogeneity, revealed diverse purchasing behaviors. These subgroupings were primarily subject-oriented with a secondary emphasis on media type.

Market segmentation was accompanied by three important technical trends--the proliferation of the PC in the workplace; the development of a CD-ROM-based marketplace; and the ability to merge ASCII, image, and sound in one medium. According to the Department of Commerce, sales of individual workstations increased 40% during the last year and will continue to soar at a rate of four times that number over the next five years.

The rapid rise of the number of CD-ROM products can be traced through a study of the Cuadra/Elsevier *Directory of Online Databases* and the recently introduced Cuadra/Elsevier *Directory of Portable Databases*. The 1990 editions indicate that, after 20 years of growth, 5,000 online databases produced by 2,000 database publishers are available on 650 online systems. These figures can be compared to the rise, in only four years, of CD-ROM to 1,000 commercially available titles.

The capability of merging ASCII, image, and sound all in the same medium has had a significant impact on current secondary information publishers. The lack of these capabilities had, in the past, limited products to the confines of text only. In the 90s, the database publisher can either expand the product definition to include images and sound or make a decision that text only is appropriate; however, a decision must be made.

Two other developments have been (1) a tremendous change in the way individuals access information and (2) a change in who those individuals are. Enter the end users. End user searching, however, does not replace the intermediary but, rather, redefines the intermediary's role as an information consultant.

Although the availability of a variety of access tools to end users certainly gives credibility to Mick O'Leary's description of the 90s as the Age of Access, database content has not expanded, in turn, to meet the needs of end users. Despite the availability and increased capabilities of the media, the preponderance of files offered on CD-ROM contain bibliographic records, presented in much the same way as in print or online.

Database publishers will continue this trend with CD-ROM for some time because of the relative ease of adapting A&I databases to the new medium and the desires of the marketplace. It is economical to continue in this fashion and; lacking a clear signal from the marketplace demonstrating the desire for other formats, the database producer sees this as the most appropriate decision.

On the other hand, as those who have gained some experience with CD-ROM know, the end users' needs are quite different from those of the intermediaries who were the initial online marketplace. The emergence of end users creates the "push-pull" environment of the marketplace. Database publishers are "pushing" the new end users to relate to databases and systems as intermediaries traditionally have, i.e., to appreciate the "value" of information; end users are "pulling" information providers to accommodate their needs, i.e., provide an answer to a question. These forces will create the crucible in which content and delivery will be destined to change, probably to diversify to fit special needs for specific markets.

Tailoring Production Systems for End Users

Developing a production system that can accommodate ASCII, image, and audio formats will be necessary for database publishers to compete in the 90s. This system will also have the capability of producing output in every available medium.

Virtually all database publishers are creating their databases using some form of automation that, at best, combines interactive capabilities with batch processing. A new generation of hardware and software is opening doors. A tremendous amount of power is now available at each workstation giving individuals in the record-building chain the capability to access and move rapidly bits and pieces of the building blocks. The abilities to browse, call, and insert from authority files; to define and move blocks of text; and to identify and propagate fields of data collectively create the possibilities of faster, cleaner, and more economic throughput.

Database publishers must be cautious; data preparation is still an intellectual process. Many decisions are made by editors, indexers, and production personnel. Automation also allows the increased capability of processing significant errors under the guise of processing cleaner data.

The possibility of building a production system complementary to the systems that the marketplace is using has occured and will continue to occur in the 90s. As the customer base increasingly uses PCs linked to databases on mainframes or networks, database publishers are beginning to move production staff to workstations, connected via LANs to mainframes, CD-nodes, printers, etc. In addition to being able to produce products, the database publisher, by design, will be able to gain working experience with the same systems that the customer base is using. The production system that is flexible enough to accept keying, scanning, electronic input, ASCII, image, full text, and special characters at the front end must also be capable of producing print and multi-media magnetic and optical formats at the back end, in addition to extracting defined fields within a record and creating indexes, directories, and special collections specific to the requirements of the end user.

At the heart of the process, the format in which data are processed--the fields and subfields, and the manner in which they are identified and arranged--will not change drastically for some time. Rather, the change will come in an altered focus, which will be on capabilities that accelerate the input process and make the output process more efficient and varied.

Product Development In The 90s

The basic physical components of an information product are the database content, the media, the channels of distribution, and the software interfaces. A fifth, not-so-silent group of components is the external factors of which the marketplace is one.

What's In The Product?

The initial stages of market segmentation spawned by acceptance of online and CDs in the 80s, combined with the more widely available, technically sophisticated, access tools of the 90s, will cause database publishers to examine the content of their products.

The content of currently available databases falls into several categories. For database publishers that support professional organizations, content goals are preliminarily defined by association missions. Core material for BIOSIS is biology; PsycINFO, psychology; Sociological Abstracts, sociology; and so forth. Other databases mimic a long-standing, successful print directory such as the *Physician's Desk Reference, Peterson's College Database*, or *Reader's Guide to Periodical Literature*. Still other databases/services contain the full text of a single publication or group of related publications such as NewsNet, Dow Jones News/Retrieval, and VU/TEXT.

The emergence of full text has probably been, however, the most significant factor affecting database publishing from a content point of view. Even if an organization publishes information that appears ill-suited to a full text model, it most likely will need to address the full text issue in the 90s. Every publisher will be prey to the market demand for currency and broader coverage which is being driven by the daily electronic delivery of full text newspapers.

Some change is already evident. IAC is combining abstracts and full text, developing niche files from its main files to form the Health Reference Center, and segmenting general online files into specific files on microfilm and CD-ROM. The content of some files, such as those found in the Health Reference Center, is being further refined by the incorporation of lay language abstracts, rewritten to simplify medical data for the end user.

University Microfilms International is combining text with image on CD-ROM by adding the abstract databases in ASCII from ABI/INFORM to their full text, image counterpart in the Business Periodicals Ondisc product. BIOSIS is offering tailored files on floppy disks. Lotus One Source is drawing from several files to mix text and numeric data in a format that parallels logical thinking patterns of its current marketplace. Each of these publishers is taking the initial steps necessary to combine the technical delivery tools available with greater knowledge of the end user, reshaping database content to fit.

Expanding the Universe of Source Materials

Once publishers have taken these initial steps--carving out portions of current databases, adding new information, and targeting subsets of current or tangential marketplaces--are there other traditional information sources available?

One source option is to encroach on the territory of another database. This approach is risky. To extend market position by processing new source material may dilute the value-added attributes by attempting to apply common philosophies across too wide a subject coverage. One also risks the marketplace's perceiving the offering as a "me too" product, especially if it has no competitive advantage over existing files.

Another strategy is to expand the universe of source materials beyond traditional sources. The database publisher may review the markets it wishes to serve and incorporate other services and/or source materials that fit the market's demands. These materials could include non-print media, such as film, audiocassettes, or PC-based information or non-traditional print sources such as government publications and unpublished documents.

For this expansion to occur, the database publisher must build a greater service orientation into the operating philosophy by entering the "push-pull" environment and developing services to suit the requirements of the "push-pull" players. The publisher on the supply side of the equation (pre-90s) will then evolve to become the information publisher of the 90s oriented to the demand side of the marketplace.

Collecting Source Materials

The publisher's task of selecting and collecting source materials will carry greater import in the 90s. Some database publishers have already recognized the importance of expanding their content while maintaining the quality of the material cited and have begun to expand their front end staffs to accommodate this task.

In addition to clerical staff, who take out subscriptions, or professional staff, who have subject-specific expertise with which to cull material within a subject area, other professionals have joined the world of acquisitions. Acquisition personnel now include staff who possess professional purchasing abilities and are able to negotiate contracts with primary publishers. When information publishers begin to view their databases as products, the need to hire persons to acquire the parts that go into making that product will be evident.

The users' needs and content missions are still important source collection considerations. Availability of source material is also a factor. If an obscure and unobtainable document is being considered for inclusion in a database, but document delivery will not be a possibility, a decision must be made whether or not to include the document at all.

In addition, there is a cost involved in collecting source material. It is hoped that databases will never be subject to the same constraints as some "complete guides" in which only those facilities who choose to advertise in a publication are included. Database publishers, however, need to apply a realistic acquisition budget to the materials collection process.

Working with Primary Publishers

A close, positive working relationship with the original publisher--the source of the material--is a key to survival in the 90s. Historically, secondary publishers have obtained material, with or without permission from primary publishers, and applied extra value to it through the abstracting and indexing process.

Several variables are changing this approach. First, primary publishers are becoming more aware of the aftermarket for their publications. They will be seeking greater control, or at least a greater understanding, of this area. While primary publishers have not appeared unduly concerned over the inclusion of the original abstracts in print or online secondary information versions, they seem to be more attentive to the availability of abstracts on CD-ROM, perhaps because of the abstracts' availability to a larger population.

Second, as full text is increasingly sought for inclusion on secondary information products, contractual agreements will be necessary. A rise in the number of secondary publishers who request the receipt of information electronically will also require a formal agreement.

Several experiments are currently underway in which primary publishers, themselves, are developing electronic publications. The National Library of Medicine is testing online updates to a printed book. This approach eases the tremendous costs and lead times needed to produce and publish updated editions in step with the rapidly changing medical specialties.

Image Premastering Services, in cooperation with the American College of Radiologists and the Mayo Clinic, is expanding its disk-based radiographic storage and transmission system to serve as a radiologic textbook. This system, which since 1983 has functioned as a real-time distribution system of x-rays, magnetic resonance images, CAT scans, and ultrasound, uses a 12-inch optical storage disc for the high-resolution images and a

CD-ROM for storing and indexing patient and diagnostic information. The same magnification and reverse image capabilities that enable diagnosticians to make accurate assessments will allow radiology students to learn diagnostic techniques from an actual image instead of a two-dimensional textbook.

In addition, many departments across all disciplines within universities are exhibiting the initial efforts toward publishing electronic papers and/or articles. Ziff-Davis is offering both print and electronic versions of a few titles. South Eugene High School in Eugene, Oregon recently produced its yearbook on CD-ROM. Included with the traditional visuals are audio features and a talking, graphic character who leads the reader through the menus. It may be difficult to sign, but years later this yearbook will be fun both to view and hear meaningful events from high school memories.

Clearly, the universe of information sources available is infinite. During the 80s, a plethora of subjects appeared as databases--from chemical compounds to cows. During the 90s, the database subject specialization will continue, and the effect on the information industry will be that marginal revenue producing databases will be cease. "This trend toward smaller, more efficient organizations also will have an impact on the information industry."[3]

Although the needs of the professional librarian as determiners/marketers of information content is paramount, other valid parameters for content development are relevant as well. The publisher in the 90s should set goals; understand the environment; segment the market; research, analyze, and revise plans; know the information industry; assess the competition; set tactics; and commit final plan to paper.

Is the Sum of the Parts Greater than the Whole?

The intrinsic value of information is not solely the information, itself, but also the end users' ability to make use of that information. Often developing a product devoted to a particular subject area--in effect performing a portion of the customers' searches prior to their accessing the database--is more valuable than a product which contains data about every possible subject.

Slicing and Dicing

What seem to be overused buzzwords in information product development--slicing and dicing, remain the most appropriate. Once the overall content is determined and expanded, information products that address a specific end user need (either as the complete database, a stand-alone subset, or in combination with complete databases or subsets from other sources) can be defined.

Subsets

A subset of a database may be as broad or as narrow in scope as the marketplace requires. Databases can be subdivided by limiting the subject matter as in *Excerpta Medica CD: Cardiology*, which includes citations and abstracts covering cardiology, cardiovascular diseases, and cardiovascular surgery; by limiting the number of years covered as in *MEDLINE* subsets; or by meeting the needs of the target audience as in *METROSCAN: Sacramento County, California*. B-I-T-S (BIOSIS Information Transfer System), a customized search from BIOSIS Previews distributed monthly on floppy disc or magnetic tape, has an even narrower focus.

Cooperative Databases

Subsets of databases combined with all or parts of related databases can satisfy information needs in a specific subject area. This offering may simply compile and configure information from disparate databases for niche markets or "wrap" it in combinations of (1) digital and analog storage; (2) optical, magnetic, and tape media; or (3) text, image, or sound output.

AIDSLINE contains information from MEDLINE, HEALTH PLANNING AND ADMINISTRATION, and CANCERLIT. U.S. Pharmacopeia is producing a product with Auburn University that uses text, graphics, and photos to instruct patients about certain medical conditions and care procedures. The patient views a customized, instructional segment that has been preprogrammed by a physician; menu items can be selected to provide audio instructions befitting the age and educational level of the patients.

Kibirige makes a case for the inclusion of full text articles in electronic delivery systems as being the most viable product of the 90s. Locating the source of information is only the first step in the searchers' quest; without the original full text document, researchers are back to square one.[4]

A study performed by CMC Research Inc. demonstrates the importance of combining full text delivery with A&I databases.[5] UMI/Data Courier and IAC not only deliver full text articles but also bundle their products with workstations to provide end users with complete systems.

Meeting User Needs

The most effective way of determining users' needs is to ask them, which is not exactly easy. Polling the marketplace about its reactions to an existing product is relatively simple; however, directing searchers to respond to a product about which they know nothing, delivered on an unfamiliar medium and including information for which the value is unknown, is somewhat trickier.

Group meeting product reviews followed by one-on-one interviews are probably the most effective method of assessing an individuals' information needs. The group meeting allows individuals to become familiar, in a general sense, with the product offering, while the individual interview can elicit more honest responses. The group meeting can also inform the interviewer about how individuals and departments relate to each other within a unique, corporate culture. The basic question is, "What information do the users need in order to make decisions?"

Information products should be designed to meet end users' goals; if their goals are increased productivity, supply users with technical information; if the primary goal is problem solving, provide tactical information; if quick decisions need to be made, furnish appropriate strategic information. DowVision was developed to address customers' information needs and to accommodate expanding technology; it offers required information, reasonable fixed-fee pricing, timeliness, redistribution capabilities, adaptability to existing systems, ability to customize, ease of use, quality, and integrity.

The size of the market for an end user product must also be measured. In addition, the longevity of the end users' needs and, therefore, the durability of the product are important considerations. Should a database publisher launch a "hot product"--the "Pet Rock" of databases?

Does the anticipated market have the appropriate hardware to support the intended product? If the answer to this question is "no," or if the expected end user group includes small organizations or individuals unable to support fully trained computer staffs, bundling a ready-to-use system with the information product may make the product more marketable. Although primarily a marketing issue, bundling has become a product development option of the 90s. In addition to the UMI and IAC systems, CD-PLUS also includes hardware in its medically oriented workstation.

Gateways can also provide a friendlier interface for online users. Lehigh University decided to distribute its local database, ASA, on a gateway. In selecting the Bell Atlantic Gateway from Bell of Pennsylvania, Lehigh University chose a service that (1) was affordable (at only $3.00 per hour); (2) serviced a densely populated area that had a higher than national average of PCs with modems and included the majority of Lehigh University alumni; (3) offered regional exposure with a small amount of risk; (4) provided marketing support; and (5) had already made inroads in the work-at-home market. A side benefit was to promote Lehigh's document delivery service.[6]

Lehigh recognized that the end user market of the 90s will include a greater number of computer literate individuals and more work-at-home personnel. Further, some information forecasters predict that the traditional information approach--browsing through library shelves--will be replaced by a small research/resource area where patrons or information consultants will locate source materials that are then delivered electronically.

This scenario, in essence, is that of a consortium warehouse proposed for the metropolitan Washington, D.C. area. Comprised of members from regional colleges and universities including Georgetown University, George Washington University, George Mason University, the University of Maryland, and the Northern Virginia Community Colleges, the consortium warehouse would house a collection of books, journals, periodicals, and other library materials. The stacks would be "accessed" by remote terminals on which patrons could identify material needed. The material would then be retrieved by a librarian (or robot) and delivered to the end users.

Developing a product for the 90s requires constant reevaluation. The universe of information is constantly expanding; the media are improving; new distribution channels are evolving; and user interfaces are moving toward intelligent systems. As the puzzle pieces change, products should not remain static. They should be revised based on users' feedback, competitive products, and advances in available technology.

Information Media: Yesterday, Today, and Tomorrow

Once the appropriate content has been selected, decisions about the appropriate delivery media for the product must reflect both the production aspects and the end users' needs. The most cost-effective and efficient medium, from a production perspective, may not have a complementary market if the end users lack the hardware to access that medium. Early CD-ROM producers gambled that the product content would drive the purchase of CD-ROM readers; their gamble paid off, but that might not always be the case.

The issue for information product developers in the 90s is not only the selection of the most appropriate medium, or media, for their products but also the added challenge of finding the appropriate fit for a product in a multi-media environment. Often keeping pace with new technology creates a challenge of its own.

Further, if database publishers find the different distribution media confusing when they, at least, have been exposed to the various forms, the end users who must deal with this information, as well as the hardware and access software information, may be totally at a loss. These novice information consumers will be bombarded with such terms as gigabyte, terrabyte, hypermedia, baud rates, etc.

Although database publishers are likely to continue following technology's lead in planning product development and expand their markets to end users, these publishers must also keep abreast of new developments and assess them in terms of applicability to the information they produce. For example, the publisher of an A&I database might envision no immediate application of audiotext or videotext; however, if expansion of coverage from journal-based to tape or film becomes a possibility, the best representation of each of these media may be in the media, itself.

This section will describe the distribution formats/media available; examine the advantages and disadvantages of each; and discuss the applications appropriate to each medium as well as future developments. Output formats such as text files, audiotext, and videotext will also be explored. Finally, combinations of distribution formats and output formats in the form of hypermedia will be discussed.

Historical Retrospective

Beginning in the 70s, the marriage of improved computer and advanced telecommunications systems created an atmosphere ripe for the introduction of online information. Lockheed Missiles and Space, System Development Corporation, Pergamon, and Bibliographic Retrieval Services, along with those institutions who had systems sophisticated enough to handle local distribution, were among the first to apply these new technologies to the distribution of information. The distribution outlets were, however, comparatively few; the access mechanisms complex; and the use limited to the experienced professionals who could navigate these systems.

The 80s heralded increased distribution outlets as a result of the proliferation of PCs; simplified, if not simple, search mechanisms; and, through the advent of CD-ROMs in the latter part of the decade, information delivery directly to the end user. The majority of these products, however, perform as if they were miniature online services.

The products of the 90s will be enhanced by improved technology and user interfaces. Likely developments include gigabit transmission and storage (ISDN); natural language interfaces; integrated, transparent access to local and remote resources, both internal and external; increasing reliance on full text material; and improvements in probabilistic, as well as boolean and pattern recognition, search capabilities. Customized online databases, real time storage, and transmission of images and animation will augment the database publisher's ability to meet end users' needs. Technological innovations will be characterized by a heightened performance at a reduced cost and system size.

Types Of Media

The media appropriate for dissemination of information fall into three categories: the traditional forms of paper or microfiche; the popular electronic forms of magnetic tape, CD-ROM, or diskettes; and the esoteric forms targeted to specific niche markets such as facsimiles, electronic mail, or optical cards.

The "Traditional" Media

Print

Despite predictions to the contrary, as well as the continued development of alternative media forms available to publishers, the paperless society has not yet become a reality. Although publishers have experienced a decline in print subscriptions, reasons other than the availability of an electronic equivalent are responsible. Increased subscription costs and decreased library budgets have also contributed to their diminution.

There will, nevertheless, always be a market for print information products. The new end users discussed earlier do not necessarily represent converted old end users. The commonly accessed print versions of dictionaries, thesauri, telephone books, and specialized sources such as *Books in Print* or *Peterson's Guides* are not destined to disappear in the 90s.

Microfilm/Microfiche

Computer output microfilm (COM) devices convert computer output to rolls of microfilm or microfiche at a speed of up to 30,000 lines per minute. A single roll of microfilm can store approximately 2,000 pages of print and costs half of its print equivalent to produce. Microfilm products require nothing but a low-cost reader to use; the reader may or may not include a printing device.

Microfilm and microfiche are still the most appropriate media for high frequency distribution to multiple locations where archival capabilities and price are of primary importance and search requirements are minimal.

The Popular Electronic Forms

Magnetic Tape

Although the first mainframe computer--UNIVAC I--was made commercially available in 1954, secondary storage devices such as the magnetic tape were not generally available until the early 60s. The tape consists of a magnetically coated surface onto which data, represented as a combination of 1s and 0s, can be recorded or rerecorded.

Magnetic tape can store approximately 110 megabytes of data per reel (approximately 27,000 pages of text); weighs a little over 2 pounds; and has an error rate of 10^{12} and an access speed of 9 minutes from end-to-end. Magnetic tape requires a mainframe system for data storage, remote terminals for data access, and software for data retrieval.

Most information publishers can easily produce a magnetic tape from existing systems as data are already being collected on a magnetic system. Access software is readily available as are distribution channels.

Magnetic tape is not, however, permanent; data can be erased or written over; access speed is compromised by the tape's having to be read in the order data are written; and the shelf life is short--approximately six months. The existence of multiple standards often requires programming time to create a tape compatible with the end user's system.

For publishers and end users without systems in place, purchasing hardware to read magnetic tapes, establishing a network for accessing tapes, and developing software for that accession can be costly ventures. In addition, these systems require information scientists to operate and maintain them.

As there are no cost savings in producing multiple tapes (other than a quantity discount in purchasing the blank tapes), magnetic tapes are the most appropriate medium for low runs of like data and application to those channels that can handle only magnetic tape.

As in the past, hardware for magnetic media will continue to decrease in physical size while increasing in capabilities. Advances in image and sound storage will also be achieved as well as improvements to software interfaces, including extensive hypertext capabilities. Unlike the same developments with optical disks, however, storage capacities and compression ratios are not advancing rapidly; the maximum storage capacity for magnetic media is 6,250 characters per inch.

CD-ROMs

The earliest optical storage application appeared in the 50s but required a massive laser and a room full of computers to operate. Throughout the next 30 years, RCA, Philips, and SONY were at the forefront of developing a compact, cost-effective format using miniaturized lasers to produce a viable consumer product.

In the early 80s, Laservision enjoyed a brief success but was shortly outpaced by SONY's Betavision and Panasonic's VHS with their expanded capabilities such as the ability to record as well as view. At the same time, SONY and Philips developed a successful optical disk application for the recording industry; and, in the mid-80s, CD-ROM (compact disc, read only memory) became available. The slow to burgeon CD-ROM medium represented a $500 million market in 1989 and is expected to quadruple that market within the next two years.

Basically, CD-ROMs store data in a binary format, i.e., as 1s and 0s, arranged spirally from the center in grooves and flat spaces. The way in which the light from the laser is scattered or reflected translates into digital signals that are interpreted by the PC and

17

coupled with Microsoft extensions (MSCDEX). The extensions allow PCs to overcome the disk operating systems' file size limitations and to access the CD-ROMs.

A CD-ROM disk can store approximately 680 megabytes of data (approximately 270,000 pages of text, 10 magnetic tapes, or 1,500 diskettes), weighs 1 ounce, and has an error rate of 10^{13} and an access speed of 1-10 seconds.

To function, CD-ROMs require a PC; a CD-ROM drive, an interface board (either SCSI or CCSI) and a cable; Microsoft extensions; and a software interface. To handle the increased space required by expanded interface capabilities, a fixed PC drive is also becoming a necessity.

CD-ROMs are reliable, permanent, and durable. They allow for direct end user access and offer unique capabilities that encourage the development of new information services. They are "sexy." Often the motivation to purchase a CD-ROM product and the supporting hardware is nothing more than the desire to be in sync with the latest technology.

CD-ROMs held another, particular appeal for the marketplace--they offered online capabilities at fixed fee (predictable) pricing. Database publishers have begun to reevaluate their pricing philosophies for CD-ROMs; and subscription fees based on output or potential use, i.e., variable pricing schemes, are once again being considered.

During the 90s, CD-ROMs will be faster, store increased amounts of data, be writable, and include multimedia functions. These changes, however, will be progressive, as CD-ROM producers cannot afford to abandon or replace the existing archival products. CD-ROMs are not the ultimate panacea for data distribution. CD-ROM drivers are slower at data transfer than their PC-fixed disk counterparts. Some standards, such as the High Sierra format, have been developed to ensure the viability of CD-ROM products, but the lack of additional standards may inhibit overall CD-ROM production.

Controllers and interfaces vary from drive supplier to drive supplier; often a CD-ROM that can be read by one drive is incompatible with another. This compatibility issue is particularly evident in the Japanese market. CD-ROMs also have a comparatively lengthy processing time, including premastering and mastering, in comparison to the almost immediate production process of magnetic tapes. "No CD-ROM is perfect; compromises are necessary to balance features, information, and the budget."[7]

The advent of CD-ROM blurs the publisher-vendor boundaries and allows database publishers to respond to vertical markets. Data can be created, packaged, and delivered without the middleman.

Diskettes

PCs (and thus diskettes) have gained significantly widespread industry acceptance. In 1988, PCs and workstations held 65 percent of the market share for computer hardware, well ahead of minicomputers and mainframes. A typical diskette can store approximately 1.2 megabytes of data (approximately 270 pages of text), weighs a little over half an ounce, and has an access speed of around a quarter of a second.

Diskettes share some of the advantages of other magnetic media, such as ease of production and availability of appropriate hardware in the marketplace. They also share optical media's increased cost savings with an increased production volume. What they do not provide is large storage space or durability.

Currently, diskette products fall into three categories: (1) well-defined full text delivery such as *Mark Twain* and the multiple user manuals produced by Electronic Test Corporation; (2) demographic studies that combine text and numeric databases for a limited region such as those published by CACI Marketing Systems and Center for Continuing Study of the California Economy; and (3) selected dissemination of information (SDI) products such as B-I-T-S, or ERIC MICROsearch.

Due to their size limitations, diskettes are not appropriate vehicles for larger databases or information products with many graphics. In addition, although some of the earlier hurdles of multiple operating system formats have been overcome, there remain large numbers of operating systems, variances in diskette sizes, and, more importantly, differences in access software.

The Esoteric Forms

Facsimiles/Electronic Mail

Although it was originally developed in the 70s, telefacsimile is not widely used because of its cost and incompatibility among telefacsimile units. In the 80s, however, telefacsimile became one of the most popular delivery mechanisms for full text documents. The almost instantaneous transmission of articles expedited document delivery faster than the U.S. Mail and cheaper than next-day delivery services.

Facsimiles are paper- and page-based delivery mechanisms that can transmit both text and images. They require only a telephone line and a facsimile system. The recent development of specialized telefacsimile boards for personal computers has further increased the efficiency of delivery. The sender can queue documents electronically; the need for a paper-based original document is eliminated.

SIMBA FaxTrax, a product of SIMBA Information, Inc., delivers business and professional information via telefacsimile. Following telephone interviews with end users, an intermediary performs a search and sends the results via facsimile.

Direct telecommunications via electronic mail (EMAIL) interacts with the end users' PCs via modem. EMAIL requires a PC, a modem with communications software, and a telecommunications service. It is predicted that the number of EMAIL messages will be 16 billion by 1992 and will increase at a rate of 30 percent annually throughout the 90s.[8]

In addition to document delivery, facsimiles, and EMAIL are appropriate choices for distributing smaller amounts of information that must be updated frequently. Information distributed on facsimile should have a short life span (i.e., read and discarded) as subsequent retrieval of the information is not efficient. Although more searchable than facsimiles, with the aid of full text search software or by saving electronic documents in a subject file, EMAIL is also suitable for delivery of read-and-discard data.

Optical Cards

Although there are no optical card products currently on the market (the first release is scheduled for April, 1991), its write-once-read-many capability is ideal for storing personal databases such as medical histories, identity verification, or automobile maintenance records. An optical card can store approximately two megabytes of data per card (approximately 800 pages of text), is about the size of a credit card, weighs less than half an ounce, has an error rate of less than 10, and costs about three cents to produce.[13]

The medium is not effected by either magnetism or static electricity. Information can be stored as either alphanumeric characters, audio, photographic, fingerprints, or signatures. Optical cards require the same equipment as CD-ROMs, except that, rather than a CD-ROM drive, an optical card reader is used.

Output Formats

Text

The most common and oldest form of database output is text--a combination of alpha and numeric characters arranged in either a relational or object-oriented database, a collection of full text documents, or both.

Audiotext

Audiotext has primarily been used for voice response applications such as that used by the telephone company when relaying a telephone number through "information." Other applications include bank inquiries for account balance information and audible feed-back from sensors to the visually impaired.

Generally, audio response is composed from a prerecorded vocabulary of frequently used words associated with the commercial or industrial applications that apply. An inquiry is received by the audio device and sent to the computer. The inquiry is then evaluated, and an appropriate, digitally coded voice message, constructed by the computer, is sent back through the audio-response system.

Speech synthesizers also allow the computer to "talk." These systems are based on predetermined patterns of speech called phonemes, which produce the sounds of the spoken word. A third form of audio output, which is not technically considered "text," originates from recorded sound. It incorporates the same technology used in producing audio CDs.

Audiotext applications for database publishers are rarely singular applications. Except in the case of direct information databases such as the telephone directory, audiotext usually appears in conjunction with text and visual media such as Britannica Software's *Compton's MultiMedia Encyclopedia*. Audiotext is also used for 900-number services wherein prerecorded messages respond to digitally input questions.

Videotext/ISDN

The high cost of mounting videotext systems has, thus far, restricted its use to commercial applications. Videotext requires an ordinary television set with a decoder/receiving device and a microcomputer for downloading the material received. Two noteworthy videotext products do, however, exist. The first, Distance Learning Network, a cooperative venture of Lehigh University, Bell of Pennsylvania, and AT&T, is a truly, interactive video network.

The other, perhaps the best known and most published videotext system available in the United States, is the IBM/Sears PRODIGY service. To quote their own marketing slogan, "The PRODIGY service makes your home computer a personal resource for information, shopping, and entertainment. If you've just been using your home computer for word processing, games, or spreadsheets, you don't know the half of what it can do for you and your family." With this product, IBM and Sears are luring end users into the information world by providing ready access to information that is commonly sought on a daily basis--consumer information, travel reservations, financial assistance, current events, and electronic mail. By offering the service at a low, fixed monthly rate, they are providing this information without the stigma of the online pay as you go pricing, and any additional fees are clearly attributed to the database producer (e.g., the bank charges a service fee for direct banking). IBM and Sears estimate that their service will have 10,000,000 subscribers by the end of the 90s.

Gregory Gerdy suggests, however, that there is a long list of end user frustrations associated with videotext--needing a modem, buying and using communications software, choosing a service, navigating the maze of commands, worrying about running up connect time charges (when applicable), hoping help lines are free--just to mention a few.[9] This evaluation may make some preliminary market penetration statistics appear optimistic.

Integrated Services Digital Networks (ISDN), like videotext, use already established telephone lines. ISDNs are able to deliver data, video, and images over standard digital telephone trunk lines; but, unlike standard videotext systems that require a PC and modem, ISDNs require only a dedicated terminal.

Currently, the largest ISDN system is the French Minitel Services Company. A joint venture of France Telecom and Infonet, Minitel emerged as a result of France Telecom's desire to supplant the printed telephone book with an electronic version. The two companies provided customers with free terminals and put the telephone book online. Once the user base was established, other members of the information industry such as news, financial, and travel information publishers were able to piggyback their products onto the Minitel service.

In the 90s, the expansion of fiber optics networks in the United States should create important information highways. U.S. West, a regional Bell operating company, has recently supplied its Omaha, Nebraska subscribers with ISDN terminals in an effort to emulate Minitel.

Adapter boards have been developed that can convert a PC into an ISDN terminal in the same way boards were developed to allow PCs to mimic telefacsimiles. This capability eliminates the need for an end user to have a dedicated ISDN terminal for information seeking in addition to a PC for other functions.

Putting It All Together--Multimedia

A multimedia system can create, import, integrate, store, retrieve, edit, and delete two or more types of media materials in digital form such as audio, image, full-motion video, and text information. According to Bailey, there are four basic types of multimedia systems--hypermedia, multimedia databases, multimedia messages, and virtual reality systems.[10]

The hypermedia models promise simple interconnections of heterogenous hardware, simple conversion of non-digital material, and, finally, the creation of an infrastructure wherein everyone has access. Although Senator Gore's supercomputer vision may not be achieved in the 90s or even decades beyond, open networks, satellite transmission of data, and the increased number of personal computers and video terminals will build its potential.

An ad touting the advantages of multimedia might read, "finally, a system that is all things to all people." Multimedia systems, once perfected, will be capable of handling multisensory data in a non-linear fashion. The ultimate multimedia system will analyze media materials and select, retrieve, and manipulate information from among them.

Interactive use will be possible, oriented to editing data and customizing functions in a multi-user environment. Through transparent, logical programs, end users will be able to retrieve exactly the information they need within specific time frames.

In actuality, the current multimedia systems are unstructured and confusing. They present so many choices that the users are ultimately overwhelmed. Average individuals require vast amounts of advanced instruction to use multimedia systems. Once again, the hue and cry for standardization is rising; integration of the number of disparate databases that currently exist is almost impossible in such a system. Materials created by end users through downloading of documents on multimedia systems could also result in copyright disputes. (Some speculate that such material could be considered as being jointly owned by the end users and the system.)

Pacific Telesis Group has been researching advanced telecommunications technology that, when coupled with a hypermedia system composed of word processing packages, databases, and geographic mapping programs, can link classrooms worldwide to enhance education and cross-cultural understanding. Video images of the participants are transmitted along with the educational materials, in text, video, and audio data formats. Students trained in this environment not only learn firsthand how to "hunt an alligator" but also "gain technical acumen, cultural awareness, and international camaraderie."[11]

Navigating databases on a multimedia system is cumbersome, especially with large systems. Development of more powerful techniques for parsing through the various nodes and links of the system or for systematic travel through an underlying graphic structure has not kept pace with the hardware. Efforts are, however, being made to improve multimedia systems so that they can handle multiple nodes as a unit, thus manipulating groups of related nodes as well as individual nodes to simplify the search.

Beyond Multimedia

Intelligent agent systems that monitor multimedia systems as well as capture relevant new data represent the wave of the future. Through hypermedia selective dissemination of information (SDI), these systems will be able to search and download multimedia data, manage and access personal databases, guide the analyses of data from each source, and further create new intellectual works.[12]

The NewsPeek system at MIT is a limited application of this kind of artificial intelligence. The system monitors computerized information systems from which it creates an electronic newspaper that is distributed to appropriate personnel.

Considerations for Media Selection

The simplest media decisions concern the size (number of megabytes) of the database and whether or not it should be a multimedia or text only product. The decision becomes more complex when the database publisher must also determine the potential end user market and the most appropriate media for that audience.

Other considerations include media stability--Will this technology survive the next five years?--and media acceptability--Will the end users continue to accept these media as information vehicles?

Distribution Channels

Once content has been established and the media selected, the database publisher must determine the most efficient and effective means of routing the information to the end user. Options include distributing the data through an online vendor, leasing the data to an institution via magnetic tape or a CD-ROM, distributing the data directly online, or utilizing a service bureau or gateway for either part or all of the distribution process.

Through an Online Vendor

Distribution through an online vendor is still, and probably will remain, one of the most common distribution channels for data produced by information publishers in the 90s. Online vendors offer the advantages of a ready base of proficient searchers; a plethora of related files; online support and cost predictability, if not fixed fee pricing; and familiarity to a core of end users.

Vendor systems also offer unrestricted access (i.e., 24 hours a day, 7 days a week). The publisher does not need to maintain a large, professional MIS staff to support its end users. In many cases, in which a file is seldom used or per search pricing provides a ready reference for client chargebacks, online searching on a host system is more economical than print or CD-ROM. The belief is still upheld that, in some endeavors, intermediaries searching an online system offer the best opportunity for obtaining complete, targeted information.

On the down side, online systems are difficult and costly for untrained searchers to use; there is often significant cost for a search for which there is no usable output. Online systems are inconvenient for individual use--the searcher must have access to a computer terminal, obtain a password, and know how to use the online system as well as how to search the individual files. Training for most online systems is targeted to information professionals and is less available for individuals. Documentation is often voluminous and sophisticated, intended as a reference for those who already know the searching protocols.

Many databases, themselves, are not structured in a natural way for end users. A psychologist attending a training session in the use of PsycINFO at a recent American Psychological Association convention was surprised to learn that the PsycINFO database is built from narrower to broader terms when he had intuitively, always searched from broad to narrow.

Leased Directly to the Institution

For organizations that possess large mainframe computers, a network, bibliographic file search software, staff support, and, most importantly, the need to disseminate collections of information to a large number of users (e.g., universities, corporations) leasing the magnetic tape version of a database directly from the information publisher is often a cost-effective and efficient move. Data can be distributed to many users simultaneously within an organization and, at the same time, provide cost efficiencies that subscriptions to CD-ROMs do not. Magnetic tape leases are a costly way of providing information; however, if set up correctly for a large demand, they can be the most economical choice overall.

In fact, it appears that the wide acceptance of CD-ROMs, especially in large academic libraries and the attendant increase in the number of CD-ROM users have reinforced interest in tape leases. Institutions are considering mounting tapes on systems built around an online environment within the defined service area. Prior to the online revolution a few universities did have tape leases but spun them in a batch mode, releasing results in printed form to users. Online delivery basically eliminated this type of delivery channel. With an increasing number of organizations becoming "wired," i.e., having large mainframes, PCs, and networked online information delivery from large databases stored on mainframes, magnetic tape leases are becoming economically feasible.

Directly to the End Users

The preceding descriptions of distribution through online vendors and leased tapes deal primarily with two types of media: magnetic tapes and full file CD-ROMs. Although some advances are being made for broader distribution of CD-ROM information through local area and wide area networks, these applications are still too slow (in response time, etc.) to be viable delivery channels when multiple users are involved. All of the other media in which information products are packaged are provided directly to end users or end user groups--optical discs, microfilm/microfiche, facsimile or electronic mail, diskettes, and optical cards.

Should the Database Publisher Distribute Its Own Data?

In his National Online 1990 address, Carvon Hudson predicted that "the day may come when the successful database producer may even create its own timesharing system in order to maintain product control and profit margin."[13] Certainly, the idea of database publishers as information publishers is not new. Chemical Abstracts Service distributes its own databases on the STN system as well as through other online vendors. IAC not only vends its database online but also publishes its databases on the INFOTRAC and TOM systems. In the same way that optical publishing afforded database publishers more control over their products, distributing their own information offers publishers more control over how users receive the data.

Several options for producing a CD-ROM product are available to database publishers--from creating an entire production system in-house to subcontracting the data conversion; premastering, mastering, and replication; interface software development, and even the packaging, marketing, and technical support either all or in part to an outside vendor. When contracting an outside vendor, a database publisher should assess the vendor's stability--Will the vendor survive to support the product in the future?--and analyze the vendor's product mixes--Will the vendor's other products provide a market advantage that will enhance the distribution of the database?

Interfaces

The importance of search software in product development cannot be stressed enough (*see* Chapter 2--Technical Considerations, p. 31). "Impeccably presented data from un-impeachable sources is worthless if access to them is denied or compromised because of obstacles imposed by the online system or the database producer."[14]

The more active a role the database publisher plays in this part of the process, the more certain the publisher's position will be in the marketplace. The interface should be: (1) easy to install and capable of modifying defaults to match the end userss systems; (2) easy to use but provide sophisticated retrieval features; and (3) able to solve the end users' problems while allowing customized searches. Customization features should be built into the end users' access software to help them manipulate the information in their natural problem-solving style. Documentation should include a tutorial and a written reference manual.

"If there is going to be a theme to full text database development in the 90s, surely it will involve accessibility rather than file-building."[15] Full text databases are among the most difficult to navigate. *The New York Times* (available online since 1986 through Mead Data Central) has attempted to ease accessibility for the searcher by increasing access points as far as including size of headline type as a delimiter; developing comprehensive indexing, including biographical information; and offering "file-within-file" organization. "Indexed full text will someday not be the exception but the rule."[16]

Expert systems will continue to be developed in the 90s to duplicate the knowledge and problem-solving skills of human experts in authoring search strategies. Tome Associates (London) is currently investigating a natural language interface that links commercial and in-house databases. Expand commands to locate misspellings and entry discrepancies are currently available in some databases and will become more prevalent; "behind the scenes mapping" will be the next step to retrieve all variant forms of a search term.[17] Other enhancements might include messages that alert the searcher to empty fields or gaps in coverage.

Not all of the solutions need to be high-tech. User documentation directly from database publishers as well as from online vendors should be available, and it should be simple to understand. Clear, concise statements at the outset should outline editorial exclusions.

What criteria should be applied for determining which software will "fit" the data? According to Theodore Durr, the following elements are necessary for viable search software.[18] The software:

> Must allow unstructured searching (free-text).
> Must provide for multi-word subject descriptors.
> Must include screen and report generators.
> Must not necessitate constant reference to a manual.
> Must have hypertext browsing capabilities.
> Must have field size limitations.
> Must be able to search ranges for dates and numbers, i.e., expand.
> Must include optional security features.

In addition to providing database access, software interfaces can be utilized to "block" information access allowing a single base product to serve multiple specialized markets. For example, if a CD-ROM disc targeted to pediatricians contained the entire MED-LINE database, the software could block all but those portions related to pediatrics instead of remastering the CD-ROM to include only those portions.

Other Considerations

The Lease/License as a Product Development Tool

Once the pieces of the product puzzle are assembled, there is one further consideration --who owns the data? Should the product be sold outright in all its forms such as print, audiotape, or videotape as published data? Should the product be leased for use within a defined community? Finally, should the product be licensed with redistribution rights explained in a formalized contract?

Although copyright and other legal issues per se will be covered more fully in Chapter 4, Implications, p. 91, the contract under which a product is purchased, leased, or licensed becomes part and parcel of the product. Some database publishers embrace the "own the disk but not the data" philosophy, while others require the return of the disk to ensure against its re-use.

The lease or license also serves to define the information product in much the same way as the content, media, distribution channel, and/or user interface. The license agreement defines the user community, the uses to which the results of a search may or may not be put, and the number of users who may use a given product during a specified period of time.

Lease/license contracts can impose certain limitations that can impede the sale of the product but, in turn, protect its future viability. Positioning an information product in the 90s requires attainment of an appropriate balance between the desire to protect data and the desire to distribute them.

Where Does the Database Publisher Go From Here?

This chapter has briefly described the cultural adjustments a database publisher must make to prepare itself for the 90s. It has also presented a range of content, media, distribution, and interface considerations that should be addressed in making product development decisions in the 90s. The decisions are not easy; there is no set formula. Technology neither inhibits the scope of the product nor protects the product's redistribution in adverse ways. The prospect of developing an information product in the 90s will be exciting and challenging!

References

1. Sulzberger, A.H. 1948. *Address to New York State Publishers Association*.

2. Forsyth, F. 1989. *The Negotiator*. Bantam Books. 7.

3. Hudson, Jr., C. 1990. "Looking Toward 2000: How the Electronic Publishing Industry Will Evolve." *National Online Meeting Proceedings-1990*. Medford: Learned Information, Inc. 169-170.

4. Kibirige, H.M. 1990. "Electronic Information Delivery Systems for the 1990s: An Analysis of Their Impact on Online Information Processing." *National Online Meeting Proceedings-1990*. Medford: Learned Information, Inc. 202.

5. Arnold, S.E. and L. Rosen. 1989. *Managing the New Electronic Information Products*. New York: Riverside Data Inc. 164.

6. Johnson, J.M. 1990. "ASA on the Bell Atlantic Gateway: The Lehigh Experience," *National Online Meeting Proceedings-1990*. Medford: Learned Information, Inc. 188-189.

7. Arnold, S.E. and L. Rosen. 1989. *Managing the New Electronic Information Products*. New York: Riverside Data Inc. 52.

8. Rothfeder, J. 1989. "Neither Rain, nor Sleet, nor Computer Glitches..." *Business Week*. May 8, 1989: 135.

9. Gerdy, G.P. 1990. "DowVision: The Next Generation in the Information Industry." *National Online Meeting Proceedings-1990*. Learned Information, Inc. 124.

10. Bailey, Jr., C.W. 1990. "Intelligent Multimedia Computer Systems: Emerging Information Resources in the Network Environment." *Library Hi Tech*, 29(1): 29.

11. Iztkan, S.J. 1990. "The Global Classroom." *World Monitor: The Christian Science Monitor Monthly*. May 3, 1990, 62(4).

12. Bailey, Jr., C.W. 1990 "Intelligent Multimedia Computer Systems: Emerging Information Resources in the Network Environment." *Library Hi Tech*. 29(1): 34.

13. Hudson, Jr., C. 1990. "Looking Toward 2000: How the Electronic Publishing Industry Will Evolve." *National Online Meeting Proceedings-1990*. Medford: Learned Information, Inc. 172.

14. Basch, R. 1990. "Database Reliability: The Black Box." *National Online Meeting Proceedings-1990*. Medford: Learned Information, Inc. 31.

15. Greengrass, A.R. 1990. "The New York Times: Finding Your Way Through the Full Text Thicket." *National Online Meeting Proceedings-1990*. Medford: Learned Information, Inc. 148.

16. Ibid. 147.

17. Basch, R. 1990. "Database Reliability: The Black Box." *National Online Meeting Proceedings-1990*. Medford: Learned Information, Inc. 33.

18. Durr, W.T. 1990. "The Design of Databases for and About Business." *National Online Meeting Proceedings-1990*. Medford: Learned Information. 94.

2

Technical Considerations

The most remarkable development during the past five years in the electronic publishing industry has been the blurring of the lines between producers, vendors, telecommunications networks, and users by the rapid and easy transfer of new technology. In 1985, 40 CD-ROM products were introduced; within three years, there was a ten-fold increase in the number of titles. In many libraries CD-ROM titles supplanted certain online databases.

During this time, there was also a dramatic increase in locally-mounted data tapes within the same institutions that were the heaviest online users. Network technologies demonstrated rapid growth, particularly in the educational and research environment, enabling former "users" to become "vendors." These developments bring us to the 90s, when any producer creating a valuable information resource, even the smallest operator, can expect to become conversant in the technologies of distribution as well as of production.

Software

Information providers (IPs) have been knowledgeable about software, both as users or creators of production software and as evaluators of the 3rd-party software with which their databases have been distributed. Software as a product, however, is very different from software for in-house use, even if the in-house software is created and maintained internally. Many of the technical issues discussed in the following sections concern the decisions that must be made when software is distributed with an information product.

General Requirements

The producer who seeks a vendor to distribute data has many factors to consider. Unfortunately, information retrieval (I/R) software is not usually at the top of the list, beyond a reasonable assurance that there is a suitable body of potential customers who know and use the software. Concerns about the software are likely to arise after the contract is signed and the database design process is begun.

At that time, the exact effect of the software upon the unique data becomes apparent; and, usually, there is a certain amount of compromise to make a fit. If the vendor places a high value on being able to offer the database, it may change the I/R software to accommodate the file. In general, however, changes are confined to that which can be achieved with the pre-processing programs that make data accessible to the I/R software. In either case, software remains firmly in the vendor's control.

Much of the following discussion is concerned with distribution technologies from the viewpoint of an IP that is considering offering a local online product, i.e., a database with software to be loaded and searched at the user's location. In this context, a local online database could be a CD-ROM, a microcomputer product or magnetic tapes loaded on a mainframe, or a network of computers. Some of the issues, however, particularly the software issues, will apply to the traditional IP/vendor relationship as well. Both user features and production features figure prominently. It must be remembered that user features are largely software-dependent.

User Features

The choice of software to go with a database that is distributed to a user's site is generally based on the software's user interface and special features that will enhance the particular database. This relationship is particularly important if the local online product is unique to the producer rather than being part of a vendor's offering. The emphasis on user features is sensible because the interface is key to selling the product.

There is not a very large number of information retrieval software packages available to an IP: CD-ROM software, for example, is represented by about 30 packages (of which only ten are in the majority of applications); mini-computer I/R software has about a half dozen offerings; and mainframe I/R software is represented by only two or three packages. With few exceptions, the user features are not dramatically different among the offerings; although some do have specialties. (Differences are more pronounced in such production aspects as which data formats are accepted.)

Currently, the user features that are typically offered in an information retrieval system include:

Boolean & Proximity Searching: Implies that the text is inverted, or indexed, to allow users to specify the physical relationship of terms within documents. Using Boolean logic, multiple terms can be used to locate documents in which any one of the multiple terms appears, documents in which all of the multiple terms appear, or documents in which one or more of the terms do appear and another of the terms does not appear. Using proximity operators, a user can find documents in which multiple terms appear in the same field of the document or in which multiple terms appear in a particular user-specified order. Precision in searching is harder to attain in a large, unstructured block of text than in a smaller, bibliographic record. For that reason, proximity operators are considered essential for searching full text databases because they require more precision in the response than do Boolean operators.

Field Searching: Allows a user to look for a term or terms within a specific portion, or field, of the records in a database--e.g., a search for "California" in the title field but not in the address field.

Range Searching: Allows the user to specify numeric ranges as part of a search. Numeric ranges of greater than (>) or less than (<) are usually handled--e.g., "find every document on the topic published between 1983 and 1987"; "find customers older than 55."

Complex Searching: Allows the user to build a search with multiple terms and in multiple steps. It is this feature that creates an interactive system--i.e., the user first enters a search statement, then adjusts the strategy in subsequent statements based on the results received. A brief example of interactivity would be a user entering a search term, receiving from the system a result of thousands of documents, then eliminating from those thousands all documents older than a year.

Synonym/Plural Searching: Allows a user to search any term for which a pre-defined synonym has been established. The system automatically retrieves both the user's term and the defined synonyms as provided by the IP. A plurals feature may work exactly like a synonym table with all plurals pre-defined, or it may be an algorithm in the software. An example of both features in use together follows: the user requests a search on "consumer price index"; the system finds "consumer price indexes" and "consumer price indices" and "CPI" in addition to the requested term.

Savings Sets: Allows the user to store a search and have it automatically re-run by the system upon command or at a pre-determined time interval.

Thesaurus Capability: Permits the IP to load a thesaurus on the system. The user can then access the thesaurus during a search session to help retrieve the proper terms to use in the search statement. Some thesauri will have an automatic mapping feature; if a user enters a term that the thesaurus defines as a non-preferred term, the system automatically converts the user's term to the preferred term.

Table of Contents(TOC)/Hierarchical Organization: Allows data, if properly tagged, to be presented to the user in a table of contents format or a similar "browsable" hierarchy. TOC capability is usually an alternative to regular searching and can be attractive to occasional or non-expert users.

Cross-references: Allows a user to move from document to document based on cross-references displayed in the text (frequently available in software packages at the micro level). Like the table-of-contents feature, cross-references must be marked by the IP during document preparation or when the data are loaded into the I/R software. This feature is also commonly referred to as hypertext.

Easy Movement in Display/Tagging: Offers a user the option to display all of a document and scroll through it or to display parts of a document and expand to the full document. This feature makes display of documents flexible and easy. There may also be the option to view "hits" or occurrence of the search term wherever it appears in a document. The user should be able to scroll from document to document within a list or move from document to document via cross-reference, all with single, consistent keystrokes. In many systems, users can tag displayed documents for further processing.

Integration of Graphics: Allows for the display of graphics. The graphics, as part of the database creation process, have been captured so that they can be linked to the text. From the users' perspectives, the graphics may be integrated with the text or may be requested separately whenever there is an indication in the text that a graphic exists. From the IPs' perspectives, graphics may be handled directly by the software or by exit programs that have been written specifically for the database.

Help-in-Context: Allows the user, at any point during the search, to ask for and receive help specific to the problem encountered. Help screens are expected to be precise and, ideally, can be tailored to a specific database.

Error Messages: Informs the user of a problem in the search statement. Like help-in-context, error messages should be specific to a situation--e.g., "document number too high" rather than "document request error."

Production Features

User features, as important as they are, should not overshadow other considerations. Unfortunately, database producers may become so enamored of software "bells and whistles" that the data processing fundamentals are overlooked. The fact that the software production features can make or break an information product is often neglected. Software that seems to perform well may be slowed by the updating process, or the response time may degrade badly at a certain threshold. It is crucial to ensure that whatever software is chosen performs acceptably for the type of data, chosen hardware configuration, number of users, and update cycles that apply to the database under consideration.

Since user features are quite well understood by most IP staff and since basic retrieval features are similar in most software offerings, a good place to begin evaluating software is with the production features. The following list of considerations does not apply to every situation, but some subset of these considerations will be important to any producer conducting a technical evaluation of software. There are many possible combinations of software, hardware, and application; thus, the discussion below is fairly general. A Resource List with references containing more detailed information appears in the Appendix.

Data Conversion

If any of the data to be incorporated into a database are not in machine readable format, a decision has to made to key or scan the data. Keying is simply the process of retyping the information into a computer so that the data will be in a form the computer can read. Scanning, or optical character recognition (OCR), is a process whereby text is physically passed through a machine that reads the text, character-by-character, and converts it into a machine readable format.

The advantages of scanning are easy document capture, quick access, guaranteed file integrity, information distribution, merger of documents with data, and improved work flow management. There are disadvantages as well. They include performance obstacles such as slow throughput (removing staples, handling large books, processing documents with narrow margins, etc.), the need for special monitors, the lack of standards, the diversity of fonts, and quality imperfections in scanned copy.

Scanning works best with data that are in clean paper form and conform to particular sets of characters. Intelligent character recognition systems can, however, recognize or learn to recognize, an almost unlimited number of fonts with a degree of accuracy said to be 99.9%. Although ninety-nine percent accuracy in a text page of 400 words can imply that only four words are misspelled, those four words might be critical in a search of litigation documents, dosage information, or defense weaponry.

Both keying and scanning are labor-intensive activities and relatively expensive--bound to involve decisions that weigh in-house processing against service bureau utilization. A very large database will usually be sent to a service bureau for keying simply because many organizations do not have data entry staff in-house.

Scanning of a large database in-house may be logical if ongoing updates are also to be scanned. This decision stems from the fact that scanning equipment can be operated to produce a very large volume of output by a comparatively small staff. Scanning is not 100% accurate, and, like keying, involves human intervention in the form of proofreading and post-editing.

Scanning can convert data to searchable or page image capture formats. Since most computer readable databases are searchable, data are most frequently captured as searchable characters. There are situations, however, in which it is useful to have a page preserved as a machine readable, graphic image, particularly if the page, itself, contains many tables and graphics.

Page image capture implies that each page of text is captured as a graphic whole rather than as discrete letters, words, and sentences. Page image capture is accomplished by a graphics scanner--it may be the OCR scanner (with a high-end machine) or a different piece of equipment. Page images, whether only graphics or full text pages, are delivered to users after a search has been performed.

Note: searchable capture, in relation to scanning, is often referred to as "ASCII" capture because the output from an OCR machine is converted to the American Standard Code for Information Interchange (ASCII). There are two basic forms of machine readable text, ASCII and Extended Binary Coded Decimal Interchange Code (EBCDIC). ASCII can be read by micro- and mini-computers; EBCDIC is read by large IBM-compatible machines. There are many conversion programs available to convert ASCII text to EBCDIC; conversion can be performed at any computer service bureau. If data are converted to ASCII before an I/R software is chosen, they can be converted to EBCDIC at a later time, if necessary.

Information retrieval mechanisms in the 90s will more frequently be able to handle special document attributes such as images, cross-references, and tables. It is worthwhile, therefore, to make decisions that address all aspects of data, even if other data to be used in the file are already available in less inclusive machine readable form. Planning the conversion process is when the producer should consider choosing a standard to which older data can be converted and creating cross links, or references and hierarchical headings. The best systems in the 90s will be able to utilize all of the types of data which an IP can provide.

Even when data are already in electronic or machine readable form and running on an online system, they will usually not be transferable to new software without specific programs written for that purpose. Most I/R software is built to accept a format more specific than "machine readable" format. If the data have been keyed, they may be keyed directly into this special format; but, more often a "conversion" program has been written to convert the data into the format accepted by the I/R software. If a product is being created from a variety of data inputs, a different conversion program will be needed for each input type.

If at all possible, the producer should have a small sample of data converted and run through a load program before a contract is signed so that any major problems with the conversion process are known. The software conversion process can be the most complex part of data conversion. When choosing an I/R software or service, there are questions to be asked:

> Does the software accept ASCII or EBCDIC data and does it convert data cleanly? (Some characters, particularly output from typesetting systems, need special handling.)

> What physical format will be required for data distribution--tapes, cartridges, or diskettes? Do diskettes need to be high density or a particular size? Must tapes be labeled?

> How many tapes are needed to hold the file(s)? If a database has been available in magnetic medium for a long time, it is likely that the cumulation of various production processes has made the database unwieldy. Such variety will cause problems during the conversion.

> Are images and headers in their own file, connected, or dropped to the bottom in no particular order? Is there one to a file or multiple?

What compression standards have been used?

How many characters are tables able to hold? Different software packages will have different requirements that can affect processing time and costs.

Standards

An emerging influence on database systems in the 90s is the development of an increasing number of standards. To ensure distribution of a database to the widest possible audience at the least cost, an IP should be aware of emerging standards and consider judicious adherence to those that will become commonplace within the industry.

Standards for electronic delivery of information are available from a number of organizations including the American National Standards Institute (ANSI), the National Institute of Standards and Technology (NIST), the International Standards Organization (ISO), the National Information Standards Organization (NISO), and the American Association of Publishers (AAP). Standards from such organizations are frequently assigned numbers and identified with a title containing the acronym of the standards organization (e.g., ANSI) as well as the assigned number.

There are also defacto, or industry, standards that generally arise while a technology is new. CD-ROM, for example, is governed by a set of official and unofficial standards, some of which contradict each other. This situation can be very confusing, but it does allow products to demonstrate the advantages or disadvantages of various standards.

Standard Generalized Markup Language (SGML), ISO 8879

Any business involved in data preparation will want to consider using SGML standards for data input. SGML standards may well become the standard format for data output from systems during the 90s. The advantage of SGML is that it treats the conceptual organization of data alone, independent of the ultimate appearance. SGML allows the author, editor, or anyone involved in the data production phase to define the relationship between, for example, a footnote and the order of its components, without regard to whether the footnote will be displayed in 10-pt type at the end of the book (or chapter, article, etc.) or in 7-pt type at the bottom of the page.

SGML marks text one time for multiple uses, including typesetting and electronic publishing. Once a document has been marked up, it may be passed from one data preparer's workstation to the next or from publisher to printer. Each participant in the chain will have the same understanding of the structural elements in the data and different concepts of the document in its ultimate appearance. The distribution software can then structure the output in any number of ways.

North American Tagging Rules, AAP
Available from the American Association of Publishers (which also supports SGML), AAP standards tag text in a standardized fashion. Some software can handle this format directly; other software requires a conversion program. The important requirement for conversion, however, is consistency, which the tagging rules do provide.

Microsoft Extensions (MSCDEX)
MSCDEX is an operating system that allows access to CD-ROM devices from DOS. The extensions are not available from Microsoft directly but, like DOS, are distributed by hardware manufacturers and selected vendors. Since so many systems use MSCDEX, a CD-ROM application has to be compatible with this standard. MSCDEX does not, however, work at this time with OS/2 or even with DOS 4.0; MSCDEX, alone, is not adequate for use on a network.

High Sierra/ISO 9660
The ISO 9660 standard is a formalization of the High Sierra standard for CD-ROM file structure. Both the ISO 9660 and High Sierra standards allow a CD-ROM user to purchase a single drive and operating system (such as MSCDEX) to run all CD-ROMs adhering to these standards. Although more CD-ROM products have been developed to conform to the original High Sierra standard, ISO 9660, which is very similar but less restrictive, is now the official standard. ISO 9660 was initially slow to gain acceptance because it required an updated set of MSCDEX, unavailable on older CD-ROM systems.

Multimedia CD-ROM Standards
There is a confusing array of standards vying for dominance in the world of audio/video CD-ROM. These standards include the CD-ROM/XA audio standard, Digital Video Interactive (DVI), Compact-Disc Interactive (CDI), and ISO Px64 video-conference standard. Philips, SONY Intel, IBM, and Microsoft have all endorsed the CD-ROM/XA and DVI standards which are expected to become multimedia standards by the mid-90s.

CD-ROM/XA are Microsoft extensions that allow video and audio to be interwoven with text. To use CD-ROM/XA, it is necessary to have a drive that reads the audio portion of the disk and an audio card in the PC that translates the digital data into sound. These types of equipment are not common in information markets.

DVI is SONY Intel proprietary technology that incorporates full-motion video into CDs and magnetic media at a very high level of compression. CDI is geared toward home entertainment; the CD drive connects to a television. These drives are due to hit the marketplace in the mid-90s. The multimedia CD-ROM standards are examples of industry standards that have been created to drive a market.

39

Common Command Language (CCL)/NISO Z39
This standard attempts to define the vocabulary, syntax, and operational meaning of commands that form a command language for use with online interactive information retrieval systems. CCL/NISO Z39 is modeled after existing online systems and command structures; therefore, it is a somewhat awkward fit with different interfaces. It is possible, however, to adapt some of the language to other systems. Doing so would address the complaint aimed at the proliferation of local online systems, that each one must be learned anew. With CCL, a simple feature like common names for identical commands on search systems can help alleviate the problem caused by diversity.

Windows 3.0
Rarely does one regard a brand new product like Windows or the Mac interface as a "standard." Referring to either of these products as a "standard" emphasizes the concept that interface standards are likely to occur, either formally or informally, as the 90s proceed. The wise IP will be prepared to act should an interface style become a defacto standard.

Search Engine Architecture, NISO Z39.50
This standard describes a "generic" search engine architecture that can work with a variety of interfaces. For a distributor of data on large-scale systems, this standard is one to watch. NISO Z39.50 is not yet well-developed; there are many functions that cannot be accomplished without creating subroutine calls (programs) that can then be defined to the standard. The idea of a standard for search engines, however, is exciting. If data are available on a standard search engine, any number of developers may find it worthwhile to create niche applications for those data. Gateways will thrive should this standard achieve wide acceptance.

Electronic Mail (EMAIL) ISO X.400/X.500
For certain information retrieval applications, particularly technical research and, possibly, business, EMAIL is going to become an increasingly more important peripheral, value-added component of information delivery systems. There are already users who want to send data to colleagues via electronic mail. For databases that are available on a vendor, a mail component will become more of an attraction. In the EMAIL environment, the X.400 or X.500 standards, which allow a mail system to send to and receive mail from other major systems, could become important.

Other Standards
In addition to the standards already mentioned, the National Information Standards Organization (NISO) distributes a number of standards for publishing and information services. NISO standards such as "Guidelines for Thesaurus Structure, Construction and Use"; "Codes for the Representation of Languages for Information Exchange"; or "Writing Abstracts" provide useful guidelines.

Loading/Updating

Deciding how a database is loaded and updated depends partially on the database content. Although, for the most part, this discussion concerns issues associated with "true" text retrieval systems, there are also database management systems (DBMSs), particularly in the PC arena. DBMSs and text retrieval systems are both distribution mechanisms for text, but they occupy somewhat different spheres.

DBMSs are a common way to store and access records such as catalogues, directories, and sales and mailing lists--any information that is highly structured and needs frequent, immediate (transactional) updating. With a DBMS, one can search for global information such as "every salesperson with a commission record for March of over $20,000" or search on specifics such as name. But DBMSs do not invert all of the text, cannot deal with unstructured text, and can be slow to respond. A DBMS database may be done in batches or transactionally, but the real forte of a DBMS is transactional updating.

True text retrieval systems can deal with large amounts of unstructured text, but inverting the text to make it searchable takes up a relatively large amount of computer time and storage. Text retrieval systems handle updating primarily in batch mode rather than online, in real time. A text retrieval system promotes many real time transactions to locate text; but, unlike a DBMS, these transactions do not update the record.

Text retrieval software accesses databases after they undergo a process called "loading." Although I/R systems have inverted file structures in common, loading occurs in a number of different ways. All factors being equal, the time and computer storage required to load a given amount of data can vary system to system by over 100%. On some systems, the updating process takes the same amount of time as the load process (indeed, the process is the same) while, in others, the updating process is much shorter, with a certain number of updates concatenated together and merged into the full load on a less frequent schedule.

The importance of time and storage requirements will ultimately depend on how the product is to be distributed. If a database product is being created for distribution by a vendor that not only has the software but also will take the data and load them, an IP's concern is minimal. The IP will want to be aware of the vendor's procedure, particularly the time, to ensure that the time required for loading and updating fits into the general production cycle for the database. The IP should also be tracking the updating process because, if loading is a separate activity from updating, which is frequently the case with a very large file, any major revisions to the file may involve a costly reload rather than a simple update.

When data are packaged with software, detailed specifications about the load process are important. It is particularly critical for the party that loads data to know how much computer disk space is needed for work space and how much time, which may be measured in hours, is needed for loading. There may be additional, manual (intellectual) tasks necessary to prepare the system to index text (such as establishing an internal system concept hierarchy). It is a good idea for the IP to test the loading process--try some practice runs with the software producer--to understand the true time and effort required.

If a database is directory information to be sold as a stand-alone product, the IP may be able to bypass some of these requirements by using DBMS software. At the very least, however, a DBMS with a bridge to text retrieval software should be considered. Bridging software will provide options later be to include text, graphics, etc.

Response Time

Response time is an obvious component of a search system to users; however, it is unlikely it will be listed as a feature of a software product, unless there is reason to doubt the response time will be adequate. Some software vendors provide benchmarks showing the response time against that of competing products. Whenever possible, an evaluation process should thoroughly test the candidate software, using searches that put the system through its paces. The hardware configuration on which software is tested should be exactly what will be used for the final product. It is difficult to predict what response time will be using different equipment.

The size of the file tested should also be similar to the size of the file to be eventually loaded. A detailed report of the analysis determining where the various databases reside on the storage disk or tape should also be available. There are almost always adjustments that can be made to improve response time.

If an IP already knows what standard response times are associated with various media, it will be an easier task for the IP to lead the database developer to the speediest options. For example, compression of the data (mentioned on p. 43), may reduce the number of computer inputs and outputs (I/O's) necessary to find a particular section of text. Depending on the software chosen, "tricks" may be applied to parts of the data such as posting certain phrases (name, lastname) as one entry in the index or separating some highly posted subdivision of the database (all the documents on sales) into its own sub-file so that a search for the term, "sales", quickly retrieves the entire subfile. It is worth an IP's time to learn enough about the chosen software to exploit fully such "tricks."

The most careful design will not preclude necessary, extensive pre-testing and evaluation of the full product before final mastering. Although there will have been several test files created, design errors that affect performance are frequently found only at the level of a full file. A laser disk product undergoes final testing on a simulation system that is purchased as part of a data preparation system or time-shared through a service bureau.

If a CD-ROM product is to be used on a network, an additional problem is the possibility of severe degradation in response time when more than three or four users simultaneously access the same disk. Extra effort, therefore, is needed to ensure adequate response time for the base CD-ROM product.

Compression

Computer space, not only time, is money. This fact explains why the percent of data compression achievable with a particular software is important. Compression stores text in an encrypted form, which takes up less space than the original text. Compression techniques vary and can achieve from 10% to 60% compression (i.e., text will require the specified percent less disk storage).

Compression routines can be quirky and may work better on some data than on others. Some powerful compression schemes can also take longer to de-compress than others. Being aware of the impact the compression process has on response time is useful. (In general, good compression will actually improve response time if a system has a CPU with enough power.) A key question is: Can the compression be used on enough fields to achieve desirable space reduction and still perform within the desired hardware configuration?

Platforms Supported

A "platform" is the hardware on which software can be run. The key dilemma in the marriage between software and hardware is that, generally speaking, the more certainty about the equipment available to run a database and its retrieval software, the fewer trade-offs available in the design. Powerful software, with many value-added features, requires powerful hardware to work properly. The size of the market equipped with powerful hardware is limited. As a consequence, software with advanced capabilities has a smaller market; less sophisticated software, compatible with a wide range of hardware, appeals to a broader market base.

Once target markets for a product are identified, it is important to learn what hardware is being used. The software for the database must support these platforms, including the right release (version number) of the operating system and any hardware peripherals commonly used by the potential buyers. One way to determine if a software product

43

will support the desired platform is to determine if there is a software technical support representative specializing in that piece of hardware. Often software is ported, or made to run, on so many platforms that a representative cannot be assigned to each platform. A better chance for good service exists if the database resides on a machine fully supported by the software provider.

Interface Tools

Unless a database is being offered through a vendor that markets numerous local online products, thereby having a common interface within a product line, the IP might want to offer the local online site the ability to customize the interface. It is true that encouraging the use of custom tailored interfaces may contradict the idea of conforming to a standard. There are already so many interfaces available, however, that it can be advantageous to allow a customer to integrate a new product with products already running at the local site. If a database product is to be sold to organizations that already have retrieval software, newsletter/bulletin boards, or even just EMAIL, the ideal situation is often to have the database "look and feel" similar to what is already available.

The ease or difficulty of achieving this ideal will vary considerably from software to software. Some software products have interface tools available. Some can be used by a product manager; others may require the work of a programmer. If a software product has no interface-building facility, it may have built-in exits. Exits are places in a program into which another program can easily be inserted; they can be used to program an interface. There may also be restrictions in the software license preventing an IP from reselling a custom interface; these restrictions can usually be negotiated.

Software in the 90s

The user features presented earlier gave a general view of what text retrieval software is capable of today. The features that will become commonplace as the 90s evolve will depend on the latest hardware platforms and on the data, themselves. The use of natural language processing, for example, could theoretically work with any platform and would not require specific data preparation by an IP, since the technology parses straight text. Highly technical data, however, are far more likely to require, if not true "natural language" searching, "smarter searching," based on the codified nature of the text and its relation to technical thesauri.

Handling graphics, already technically feasible, is utilized little for various reasons. Data are frequently captured separately from graphics; but even if the two are captured together, the target markets are unlikely to have the equipment needed to display the images. The CD/XA standard for CD-ROM, with its compressed and interweaved audio format and standard graphics format, could make CD-ROM graphics commonplace, but, again, users would need to purchase the equipment.

In some environments, such as networks, frequently the remote communications software (commonly called RCCS) don't support graphics. A number of demonstration systems using graphics exist in a variety of hybrid ways, such as online with local CD-ROM graphics or online with faxed graphics; but, so far, the market demand for graphics is not there. It will take only one popular application, however, or a hardware breakthrough to change this situation quickly. Any IP entering the 90s unprepared to integrate graphics with products is courting inevitable trouble.

As mentioned earlier, the differences between DBMSs and text retrieval software lie in how they handle and update text. Currently, there is a demarcation between these two system types from both the technical and product standpoints. It seems likely that software that provides the best combination of all types of updating will be required in the increasingly fast-paced information marketplace of the 90s.

DBMSs with "bridges" to text retrieval are emerging. A bridge allows different kinds of data to receive different treatment while residing in the same database. The demarcation between text and numerical information will also begin to disappear in the future, as systems are built to handle both types of data well.

Hypertext, table of contents, and hierarchical document systems are already commonplace in the PC environment, partially because the labor to create these systems is more feasible on a PC-scale database. We have begun to see and will continue to see, however, hypertext, table of contents, etc., built into large-scale systems that will manipulate well-marked data to create these features without further intervention. These and other software features, such as the ability to search multiple databases as one file, will force IPs to distinguish their data from those of their competitors and employ more value-added processing.

Create, Buy, or Adapt Software?

The previous discussion implied that an IP would either go through a vendor or lease or purchase software to use in distributing a database. There is another option, taken by some: creating unique, new software. The idea has appeal for a number of reasons related to control of the product. An IP who owns its own software is free to customize interfaces and applications at will, can choose which hardware platforms to support, and can consider long-term options for expansion into online vending, software sales, and associated consulting services. The risk is that the time and costs associated with creating a new software may outweigh the benefits.

The following discussion addresses some of the less obvious effects of building new software. In general, unless an organization is prepared to change the nature of the company and committed to the long-term benefits, it should probably buy or adapt software rather than create.

Time/Cost

An organization is more tempted to create new software if there are already an in-house data processing (DP) shop and programming staff that has created previous in-house applications software. The prudent IP will scrutinize carefully the particular expertise existing in-house. If these staff are familiar with, but not knowledgeable about, the exact hardware, software, and operating systems that are planned for use with the product, the budget estimates must be adjusted to recognize this fact.

It is also important to pay attention to what the in-house staff have included in their own estimates. What was allocated for design? Was the estimate based on a marketing requirements statement? The design phase, which typically lasts the entire life of the project, will require input from a high-level marketing person for the duration of the project.

Often in-house staff will underestimate quality control (QC) needs. In-house standards, which can be lenient about system bugs, could ruin a software product intended for public distribution. If an IP chooses not to thoroughly test and de-bug a database system at the pre-release stage, the product will receive slow acceptance. Quality control will cost about one third the development time and costs (or even more, if quality control is overlooked initially).

Creation--Maintenance/Enhancement Issues

Before a new software product is publicly released, planning begins for the next release, or version, of the software, in which enhancements and fixes will appear. Taking on the creation of a software product commits an IP to an entire system of support, maintenance, and control for the software.

A software provider maintains not only a programming staff but also a technical support staff. Besides answering user questions on a range of technical issues that go beyond the immediate software to include the hardware and operating system environment of the product, technical support staff will manage the maintenance process. They will track user requests and create problem reports, track the software releases that include fixes, and track which customer has installed which release. Technical support staff may also be called on to maintain software libraries and control the integrity of the programs from release to release.

Installation/How Software is Delivered

Is software delivered alone or with data? It may seem reasonable to assume that software will be delivered to a user on a floppy disk or tape with a manual, because many microcomputer software products are delivered that way. New technologies and different platforms do, however, provide other options.

Software can be distributed on separate magnetic media; it can be sent with data on tape or disk; it can be installed directly on hardware; or it can be downloaded to the user's system. The actual installation method used will depend on a number of factors: the price of the product; the user's expectation; the production cycle; and the IP's or vendor's expertise. One must remember that options exist.

Frequently space, production, or timing considerations preclude packaging software with data. Including software with data, however, as with CD-ROMs, is attractive because doing so eliminates the need to install the software on the user's hard disk. Downloading software is an attractive option for software updates; it cuts down on paperwork and mailing and provides fast, timely service. Downloading software, however, requires a sophisticated user base, and telecommunications expertise among the technical support staff.

Those who develop the traditional tape/disk/manual package will find that all initial efforts to create the most intelligent installation procedure possible is worthwhile. The less the customers must know about installing a software product, the better. Outside of the PC MS/DOS environment, developing an installation package is easier since software is less dependent on operating system parameters in the mini-computer environment than in the PC environment.

When many software products are delivered to a large, geographically diverse user base, both the software products and their documentation are commonly sent out on CD-ROMs or DATs (Digital Audio Tapes). CD-ROM is particularly attractive because portions of the ROM can be "locked" and "unlocked," depending on the package ordered.

DAT tape is most widely used for archival data, particularly data backup. The advantage of DAT tape is reliability, combined with tremendous storage capability. An 8mm DAT tape can store 2.2 gigabytes of information; a 4mm DAT tape can store about 1.2 gigabytes (compared to 660 megabytes for a CD-ROM). There are also quarter-inch DAT tapes which can handle a gigabyte of storage and have the fastest data-transfer rates. If DAT tapes, like CD-ROM, become common as consumer music products, this technology could become an affordable option for many applications.

With a high-end mainframe system, software delivery options are somewhat different. The user expects the software provider to install the software directly at the customer site. It is usually more efficient for a user to complete the installation, followed within a week or two by a site-visit from the software provider.

This procedure demands extra effort in the pre-installation stage by the software provider. The provider must know the customer's file names and production conventions to create a tailored installation kit to send to the customer. If the site is well-prepared and can install the software, the follow-up visit will be productive for both parties.

The key ingredient for any successful installation is clear documentation. Whatever the platform, good documentation models exist. It is worthwhile to examine competitors' installation techniques.

The next most important consideration for installation is having a knowledgeable technical support staff, who will manage not only initial installations, but also distribution of upgrades. Unfortunately, all customers don't upgrade to the latest version of a software; the more a technical support unit takes an active role in initial installations and tracking upgrades, the better it can support the customers.

With a local online product, which includes data, this aspect of product control is more difficult. Customers have been known to load the latest data. Whenever a full reload of data is issued, it can be a good idea to require that old data be returned to ensure both product quality and support integrity.

Hardware

It is said that, by 1995, PCs will have the computing power of today's mainframes, a prediction that, in theory, could dramatically change the nature of information distribution. If CD-ROMs are any lesson, however, prices will not be attractive enough to convince people to replace their current equipment; networks will not provide "gateways" fast enough or soon enough; operating systems will be burdened by these supersystems; or newer developments on mainframes will cause a return to centralized processing. The point is that the "smaller, more powerful, faster" predictions being aired during the past ten years don't necessarily extrapolate to what will actually happen with new technologies, particularly in the hardware arena. As was the case with video disks, even superior technology does not always succeed.

It is likely that, in the 90s, there will continue to be a situation wherein some IPs will take a conservative approach to new hardware technology and some, who gamble on new hardware, will either hit big or fold fast. Even now, the jury is out on CD-ROM. Will writable disks make CD-ROM a footnote in data processing history?

Providing hardware is a difficult decision for most software-oriented businesses to make. Not only are the environment and level of support unfamiliar, accounting and inventory control are different with hardware. More importantly, most IP companies don't build their own hardware, thus they must provide product support for a third party. On the other hand, for a new market, there are compelling reasons to provide hardware. Doing so creates a user base with compatible equipment and controls the platforms for software development.

In the early 90s, some products seem to have plateaued at a sufficiently high market acceptance level (CD-ROM, for example) that IPs do not have to consider turnkey hardware systems. The trend seems to favor open architectures that allow multiple products and resource sharing. Whenever a new technology has arisen, however, hardware has been bundled with services or products; this trend will continue as new technologies emerge.

Bundling Hardware with Data

In general the issues involved in bundling hardware with a database are:

Price/Volume Discount
Because hardware is often bundled with a product specifically to seed the market, the IP should be able to negotiate a volume discount with the hardware manufacturer. Typically, the hardware manufacturer will insist on a guarantee of a certain volume to be sold by the IP during the first year. That guarantee will free the IP from having to inventory the whole amount of hardware; the hardware manufacturer will usually ship the stock to the IP as needed. The realistic basis of the IP's sales projections is the most important aspect of the volume discount arrangement.

Lease vs. Purchase
There are two questions relating to a lease/purchase decision: (1) Will the IP lease or purchase equipment from the hardware manufacturer? (2) Will the IP, in turn, lease or sell hardware to its customers? The cost of the product is a determining factor. In general, it is not worth the extra work involved to lease a "small ticket" (under $3,000) item. At the same time, customers are reluctant to purchase brand new technology if a lease is available.

Warranties and Maintenance
The warranty/maintenance is almost always guaranteed by the hardware vendor. The IP should avoid, at all costs, becoming the middle-man. The customer should ship hardware in need of repair directly back to the hardware vendor.

Shipping/Handling

If the hardware is small, such as a CD-ROM player, and if an IP already has an effective in-house distribution mechanism, the IP should assume the shipping responsibility. An IP has much firmer control over the presentation of a product and can avoid record-keeping problems if it handles shipping directly, not through a vendor. Maintaining the necessary inventory should be manageable for small items.

Changing Technologies

Once an agreement is made with a hardware vendor, the IP must stay abreast of changing technologies and be prepared to strike a new deal. As hardware improvements occur, the IP may want to arrange with the hardware vendor to offer a private label for a new piece of technology. Private labeling means that manufactured hardware is sold by the IP under its own brand name. Private labeling allows an IP to respond quickly to innovations in technology and to acquire a reputation for innovation.

Networked CD-ROMs

Since most databases distributed with hardware are CD-ROMs, a brief discussion of the hardware associated with CD-ROMs, particularly networked CD-ROMs, is worthwhile. The original single-PC, single-database CD-ROMs introduced in 1985 have quickly given way to multiple CD-ROM titles on networks that allow multiple users to search a CD-ROM. This rapid evolution foreshadows database requirements in the 90s.

Librarians and information professionals have discovered that, while they like the pricing and local control of CD-ROMs, they still want the broad assortment of databases and convenience of traditional online services. There are detractors of CD-ROM technology who say that what the customer is asking for is a combination of mutually exclusive technical and economic factors--the more online-like features and amenities offered by CD-ROM, the greater the expense to the customer. Despite this anomaly, the CD-ROM marketplace has embraced the networked, jukeboxed, CD-ROM products in its effort to approximate online systems locally. It is no longer possible to offer a CD-ROM product without confronting networking issues.

The problem with networking, for the IP, is that networks require substantial technical knowledge. That networked CDs are a new technology with many problems yet to overcome makes this need critical. Performance is often unreliable; solutions are not always immediately apparent. The following chapter, Chapter 3--Networking Options, provides ample detail about networks. This discussion orients the reader to the necessary research.

Jukeboxes

The first CD-ROM products consisted of a PC (usually purchased separately), a CD-ROM reader, an interface board installed on the dedicated PC so that the PC and reader could communicate, and the CD-ROM and software. The CD-ROM player and interface board were often bundled with the CD-ROM and software, particularly if the CD-ROM was the first purchase by an institution. This configuration--PC, CD-ROM player, interface board, and CD-ROM--furnished a user with every piece of equipment necessary to access one CD-ROM title.

Total satisfaction with the CD installation was not universal--users quickly realized a problem. Only one user at a time could access the title; furthermore, only one title at a time could be accessed. If more than one CD-ROM disk were to be searched, the user had to physically remove the first CD-ROM from the player and insert another. This process offered too many opportunities for lost or damaged CD-ROM disks, particularly for CD-ROMs available on the reference room floor. It also annoyed users who had to go to the librarian's station to obtain the second CD-ROM, which was often the back file of the first CD-ROM.

Jukeboxes were, historically, one of the first add-on technologies to CD-ROM to address the "one user at a time" problem mentioned above. As the name implies, jukeboxes are a number of CD-ROM readers physically linked so that more than one CD-ROM title can be accessed by the same PC. It is still true that the user can only access one CD-ROM at one time.

Local Area Networks (LANs)

Local area networks first became popular as office automation systems (see Chapter 3--Networking Options, p. 67 for further discussion). LANs consist of a cable connecting two or more PCs together and a file server, much like a computer without a video terminal. The software that controls PC access to applications programs resides on disk either in the server or attached to it. When a PC on the LAN requests access to a shared software program such as wordprocessing, the LAN sends the program to the PC and loads it into the PC's temporary memory.

Since more than one person can simultaneously access a single software package, LANs are an attractive technology for CD-ROMs. A CD-ROM network such as CD-NET or OptiNet attaches to the file server of an existing LAN; the file server then acts like another set of disk drives available to the LAN.

The network is "local" because space restrictions exist on how far apart the PCs and servers can be physically located. A LAN can extend a maximum of about 600 feet. A LAN consists of hardware (the cables; the server; and the network interface cards, NICs, which are inserted into each networked PC similar to CD-ROM interface boards) and software. Both the hardware and software are purchased from one vendor.

LANs are configured in one of three protocol types: EtherNet, Token Ring, or ARCnet. These protocols are also referred to as "backbones" because, in addition to defining the protocol used to communicate between the PCs and server, they include the cables and boards that are inserted into the PCs to connect them to the LAN.

Software applications for LANs, including CD-ROM LAN products, need to work with a particular protocol so the product can run. Compatibility with a protocol may be described either directly, i.e., "runs under EtherNet or Token Ring," or indirectly, by reference to a brand name, i.e., "supports Novell Networks."

CD-ROMs attached to LANs are further distinguished by two basic types of set-ups, the peer-to-peer network or the server-based network. In a peer-to-peer network, each PC on the network is connected directly to its own CD-ROM server through Microsoft extensions. The network allows each station to share the contents of the multiple servers. Peer-to-peer networks are common if only a few PCs are attached to the network.

Server-based networks, which are more common, consist of a tower of CD-ROM servers which is then attached through the network cables to all of the PCs on the network. Problems arise if a CD-ROM designed to work in a peer-to-peer network is used in this configuration. This CD-ROM will be expecting the Microsoft extensions to be attached to each PC; but, with the server-based network, the extensions are attached to the tower.

Wide Area Networks (WANS)

A Wide Area Network is similar to a LAN but differs in that wider access than available on a LAN (600 feet) to the network is possible. WANs use fiber optics and a mini-computer UNIX operating system protocol called TCP/IP to operate a network over greater distances.

While it is possible, it is not easy to set up a CD-ROM system on a WAN. The Microsoft extensions problem that prevents a CD-ROM running on a server-based LAN will almost certainly make it impossible to run on a WAN. If a WAN configuration is the goal, the software must be specifically designed. There are additional logistical and response time problems in this environment. WANs are mentioned in this context because customers will attempt to set up CD-ROMs on WANs, and future R&D developments may make CD-ROM feasible on WANs.

Remote Dial Access to Networks

Some CD-ROM customers would like dial access to a network. To have dial access, remote (RCCS) software must be attached to the PC or server having the modem. RCCS software often does not support graphics, and setting up remote dial access to a network containing diverse programs can be problematic. The concept of dial access to a LAN also has implications for pricing and licensing.

Hardware in the 90s

A potential direction for hardware that affects IPs is the continuing development of parallel processing hardware--hardware that is the I/R mechanism. With parallel processing, a computer is wired to process many pieces of information virtually simultaneously.

On today's computers, with classic I/R software, the text is inverted; the computer performs the steps necessary to find a requested piece of information sequentially and as efficiently as possible. On a parallel processor, the text is entered as straight text, and the processor executes simultaneously the many steps to find a particular piece of information, eliminating the need for inversion.

A start-up company is planning to develop an I/R "chip." If PCs were available with an I/R component that could handle unstructured text, the marketplace for text would become more ubiquitous. The IP may view this development as an opportunity or a nightmare.

What has prevented downloading from becoming the issue it threatened to be is the difficulty of transferring downloaded data into a text retrieval software. While data can be downloaded and moved into a wordprocessing package easily, only the most sophisticated user will retag the data for input into a DBMS or run it through one of the more complicated post-processing packages that "easily" accepts certain online formats.

Conversely, if downloaded data became automatically searchable on a hard disk, the obstacle to downloading would disappear. It seems likely that, in the 90s, such post-processing will remain a fanciful notion rather than becoming a reality. It is, nevertheless, one of the technologies of which IPs need to be aware as they add value to their data through the inclusion of graphics, numerics, and unique bundling arrangements of software and data that enhance the text beyond mere retrieval.

Another possible scenario is that, in spite of increased capacity, PCs will be used more and more as powerful front ends to mini-computers or mainframes. The success of LAN technology, regardless of the performance issues and "care and feeding" required, indicates that, as long as users can access the information they need, they don't want to load and maintain software on their own machines. The LAN trend could quickly change the platforms that are common for retrieval applications. For example, a UNIX-based CD-ROM running on a LAN can support more users than a DOS-based CD, and the possibility that UNIX systems will become more common within the corporate environment exists.

Technical Support Staff Requirements

Technical support staff are the heart of the software sales and the most visible difference between a company distributing bundled data and system and a company distributing only data. Of course, a vendor can distribute data, even in the local online arena; then the burden of technical support falls upon the vendor. Whoever is responsible for the technical support--the UP, vendor or customer--the same concerns are applicable.

Staffing Qualifications

Technical support staff are usually "homegrown." They arrive with expertise in data processing, particularly applications, and understand the market. They should be well-rounded generalists, unintimidated by technical detail and able to relate well to customers. The technical support representative will have a high energy level and enthusiasm, and often be starting a career or looking for a career change.

Because the work is fast-paced, varied, and interesting, it should be possible to attract a fairly stable group of support representatives. Staff stability is a key component of quality control for a software product.

The appropriate candidate for the technical support manager's role, particularly if the technical department is new, is a person with experience in technical support, customer services, or telemarketing, preferably with managerial experience and a data processing background.

Technical Support Tasks

In many ways the technical support team is analogous to an online customer services group; and, like customer services, its exact tasks will vary among companies. Technical support is more broadly defined, however, and will trade subject and application expertise for platform and software knowledge.

Like customer service, the primary duty of technical support staff is to provide telephone assistance for problems. Although the staff may specialize in platforms or applications, they are expected to handle a full range of problems involving billing/accounting, installation, operating system parameters, use of the system, and system bug reports. Because technical support staff work so closely with the customer, they become the conduit for complaints, suggestions, and general market information fed to sales and marketing personnel.

Internally, technical support staff play a crucial role in maintaining product records such as release data, user request files, and project tracking. In many cases, technical support staff collectively become the quality control department, the software library managers, and the software release designers. Technical support staff often play a key role in documentation, acting as both editors and beta testers. In a mainframe environment, they often serve as installers, consultants, and field sales support staff.

Physical Environment Requirements

The equipment and software used by technical support staff are fairly standard and can be easily assembled. General overhead for technical support staff is similar to customer services but will require slightly more computer equipment, particularly if a product is supported on more than one platform. A technical support representative will need to access the application system, the development system for library control and code checking, and the in-house database for call reports, user requests, and release information.

Unless a product is generic or comprehensive, the IP should equip a computer lab with at least one example of each hardware platform the product supports. If this setup is too expensive to maintain, the most commonly used platforms should, at least, reside in-house and access to others offsite should be arranged.

One last useful feature is an EMAIL system on which customers can reach technical support staff. An effective EMAIL system will also offer a bulletin board or database capability to transmit problem reports, hot tips, and news items.

Technical support staff are generally located together in carrels in an open space, rather than in individual offices. This setup encourages cross-fertilization of expertise. Care should be taken to ensure that the phone system is not too intrusive and that hardware is placed to keep movement to a minimum.

Summary

There is a vast array of software and hardware available for electronic distribution of information; each involves detailed and changing technical considerations. A general overview of the choices and issues facing an IP has been presented in this chapter. The Resource List in the Appendix is an excellent starting point for those in search of more detailed information.

The most important advice for the IP, as the 90s begin, is not to concentrate on a specific platform or application but to be prepared, in the widest sense, to utilize all available data, conform to standards, and know the strengths of the product and the added value that is possible. The IP that focuses on product and market will be better equipped to take advantage of the technology, not be driven by it.

References

Andrews, C. 1990. "Understanding CD-ROM Software." *CD-ROM Professional*. 3(62): 4-59.

Barkley, J. 1986. *Personal Computer Networks*. NBS Special Publication 500-140.

Barron, D. 1989. "Why use SGML." *Electronic Publishing*. 2(24): 1-3.

Bash, A.J. 1990. "Adventures in Technical Support: A View From the CD-ROM Trenches at Dialog." *CD-ROM Professional*. 3(32): 5-29.

Brazeau, R. 1989. "Flatbed and sheetfed scanners optimized for different applications (buyers guide)." *PC Week*. 6(1): 45-171.

Christodoulakis, S. and D.A. Ford. 1991. "Optimal Placement of High Probability Randomly Retrieved Blocks on CLV Optical Discs." *ACM Transactions on Information Systems*.

Cooper, M.D. 1983. "Response time variations in an online search system." *Journal of the American Society for Information Science*. 374-377.

Crawford, W. 1989. "Standards, innovation and optical media." *Laserdisk Professional*. 2(37): 1-31.

Evans, N. 1989. "Development of the Carnegie-Mellon Library Information System." *Information Technology and Libraries*. 8(112): 2-110.

Finnegan, G.A. 1990. "Wiring Information to a College Campus: A Port for Every Pillow." *Online*. 14(40): 1-37.

Fox, E.A. and A.M. Daoud. 1990. "CD-ROM Hardware: What's Real, What's Next." *Online/CD-ROM 90' Conference Proceedings*. 5(67): 7-63.

Grotophorst, C.W. 1988. "Squeeze and search: implementing data compression in small systems." *Library Software Review*. 7(382): 6-378.

Hane, P. 1989. "CD-ROM drives: What's available and what to look for when buying one." *Laserdisk Professional*. 2(19): 1-13.

Harney, J.M. 1989. "A Comparison of Different CD-ROM Local Area Networks in Universities." *CD-ROM EndUser.* 1(22): 2-17.

Hatvany, B. 1989. "Comparison of CD-ROM and Online." *Proceedings of the 11th International Online Infomation Meeting.* 8-10.

Kane, R.W. and T. Peterson. 1989. "Scanners Build a Better Image." *PC Magazine.* 8: 6.

Kaysen, J. 1989. "Let's play tag: the promise of SGML." *OCLC Micro.* 5(28): 5-26.

Kovarick, A.E. 1989. "High Sierra Vs. ISO 9660: A summary." *Laserdisk Professional.* 2(22): 5-20.

Lake, M. 1991. "Strentgh of Character Recognition." *Publish.* January, 1991. 62-64.

Lavoie, F.J. 1989. "Low-end scanners woo the end user." *Modern Office Technology.* 34(4): 9-96.

Leggott, M. 1989. "CD-ROM and LAN: Some Practical Considerations." *CD-ROM EndUser.* 1(28): 3-26.

Lynch, C.A. 1988. "Response time measurement and performance analysis in public access information retrieval systems." *Information Technology and Libraries.* 7(7): 2-177.

Matthews, J.R. 1986. "Benchmark and acceptance tests: why and when to use them." *Library Hi Tech.* 4(50): 3-43.

McCarthy, M. 1984. "Data Compression Techniques." *Computers and Electronics.* 2-67.

McQueen, H. 1990. "Remote Dial-In Patron Access to CD-ROM LANs." *CD-ROM Professional.* 3(23): 4-20.

Muller, C. 1989. "Using an outside source for data conversion." *Journal of Systems Management.* 40(2): 9-7.

O'Leary, M. 1990. "Local Online: The Genie is out of the Bottle--Part 1." *Online.* 14(18): 1-15.

O'Leary, M. 1990. "Local Online: The Genie is out of the Bottle--Part 2." *Online.* 14(33): 2-27.

Raita, T. and J. Teuhola. 1989. "Predictive encoding in text compression." *Information Processing and Management.* 25(160): 2-151.

Rizzo, J. 1990. "How to Set Up the Perfect Network." *MacUser*. 6(19): 6-4.

Rodgers, D. 1990. "Step-by-Step Through the CD-ROM Production Process." *Laserdisk Professional*. 3(39): 1-36.

Rosen, L. 1990. "CD-ROM Hardware Choices." *Online*. 14(124): 5-212.

Rutherford, John. 1990. "Improving CD-ROM Management Through Networking." *CD-ROM Professional*. 3(27): 5-20.

Spanbauer, S. 1991. "OCR at Work." *Publish*. January, 1991. 64-67.

Thompson, M.K. and K. Maxwell. 1990. "Networking CD-ROMs." *PC Magazine*. 9(260): 4-237.

Vanker, A.D. 1989. "Digital Audio Tape: Yet Another Archival Media?" *Laserdisk Professional*. 2(22): 5-20.

Van Name, M.L. and B. Catchings. 1990. "A Natural Match. Sharing CD-ROMs on a LAN is a natural idea, but it's still a little harder than it should be." *BYTE*. 15(112): 6-109.

Wilke, J.R. 1990. "Parallel Processing Computers Attract Crowd of Investors Despite Limited Uses." *Wall Street Journal*. Section B1.

Wisniewski, J.L. 1986. "Compression of index term dictionary in inverted-file-orientated database: some effective algorithms." *Information Processing and Management*. 22(501): 6-493.

Zaino, J. 1990. "Endurance tests: scanners and printers." *PC Magazine*. 9(16): 11-245.

Zarley, C. 1989. "DAT, Quarter-inch drives challenge 8mm predominance." *PC Week*. 6: 48-96.

3

Networking Options

An area that will stimulate much discussion in the 90s is that of the networked distribution of information. Items fundamental to those discussions include (1) the development and establishment of networks; (2) the impact that networks will have on traditional forms of networked information distribution; and (3) the planning necessary to move into this area.

Key to the database producer's understanding in this area is an awareness of the activities of various national initiatives to establish high speed, high capacity, national networks to support information transfer between and among government, research, educational, and corporate organizations. Much of the activity in the 90s will take the form of preparation for these national networks. Of special interest is the host of major policy issues to be addressed before commercial distribution of many types of information can be considered functional and economically viable. Major items on the planning agendas of the 90s will be the development of policies and procedures in such areas as property rights, pricing, licensing, and standards.

Secondary Services in the Network Arena

The role that the secondary A&I services will play in the network arena is not yet clear. Secondary service providers bring a wealth of experience to bear on the important issues of property rights, pricing, licensing, and standards; much is to be gained or lost by A&I services in future policy decisions.

The goal here is to take a marketing rather than a technical view of network opportunities for the secondary service provider. The issue for the database producer is what all of these network options mean in terms of (1) products and services offered; (2) competition from automated "indexing" systems and how these new systems relate to past and present products and charging systems; and (3) provision of copyright protection measures.

Network, library, and publishing literature, the everyday press, and a host of conferences are filled with information about the new and bigger networks being planned and constructed. References at the end of this chapter are provided for readers interested in more detail about network architecture. There are many other good books available--a library or bookstore can provide them. The references listed at the end of this chapter are representative, chosen in part because they give both a broad overview of the international situation and a close look at domestic campus activities.

Contact information is also given at the end of the chapter for various groups active in several areas of development of networked data systems. The information is included to allow the interested reader to monitor future progress or, better yet, to become involved in the activities that will shape the policies and standards being formulated.

Research for this chapter revealed that, within many development groups, there was keen interest in the networking of A&I services but that the impetus for that networking was coming from users, often non-library users, not from publishers. Networked access to secondary literature is clearly in the future. Many of the details remain to be sorted out. The 90s is the time to be involved in shaping that future.

Technical Progress vs. Market Data

Technical progress in the last decade has been substantial, but further technical development and implementation are necessary. For many, especially for the database producer, the key issues are marketing ones such as price, products, and intellectual property rights. In many cases, truly adequate answers to the marketing questions can be answered only with experience in delivery of services, detailed user feedback, and usage data. Through the avenues of prototype and development projects, such experience is being gained, and such data are being collected.

Market Demand for Networked Services

The demand for networked access to bibliographic information is being fueled from many areas. Network designers, network administrators, librarians, library donors, library patrons, other electronic products and services, and feature articles in the popular press are all contributing.

Network system designers and builders, having implemented effective network systems, now can turn their attention to the identification of content-bearing files to put up on those systems. Managers of networked administrative, research, and analytical data functions within organizations are recognizing the need for coordination of their services; in the process, they are drawing on the information community. Professionals with library, information, and publishing backgrounds are being included in planning for the coordination of network activities.

The librarian's training and experience in dealing with acquisition, control, and distribution of multiple data formats from multiple information sources and suppliers and the library's traditional involvement in issues of intellectual property rights provide much needed expertise in framing policies and procedures. The librarian's knowledge of available products and services also generates demand for the products of bibliographic database providers, as the bibliographic products are understood and appreciated in more depth by the library community than by those outside.

Electronic solutions are being sought within the library community to address information preservation and access needs--solutions that can make scholarly materials available to researchers regardless of location and that include such necessary access tools as high quality text and image content. The rising costs of subscriptions, reduced budgets, and financial and space constraints on physical expansion, all point to resource sharing and remote access solutions. Donor funding is increasingly tied to finding electronic solutions to information handling problems.

Until recently, however, electronic solutions have been limited. Networks were not of sufficiently high capacity to handle images, and distributed solutions such as CD-ROM did not allow multi-user or remote access. All this is changing, however, as high speed networks are being put into place. Users are becoming familiar with networked systems from simple electronic mail to the transfer, use, and analysis of complex data files. As users recognize the value of such services and incorporate them into their work flow, they identify and demand other services, including bibliographic access.

One type of networked library application that is creating visibility and, therefore, demand is the public access catalog (PAC). The automated PAC is replacing card and print catalogs at libraries. Users enter requests to local public and/or university library catalogs from terminals in the library or through modem connections in the dormitory, laboratory, home, or office. PAC users are becoming facile, even on rather primitive systems, at locating items of interest. These users learn to appreciate the search capabilities, the holdings information, and the circulation status that the PACs provide; they quickly take the next step of requesting that the indexing of journal contents be offered in this medium as well.

Databases on CD-ROM are also creating demand for networked services. Microcomputer based CD-ROM systems containing both text and images are appearing in ever greater numbers in library reference areas. CD-ROMs are effectively moving the search responsibility from the hands of the librarian to those of the user. Professional library staff can now pass some of the responsibility for interactive searching on to the consumer. In many libraries this shift is indeed mandated by staff and budget constraints.

As a consequence, a whole generation of new users is discovering the advantages of direct, computerized access to information. Once the CD databases are put directly into users' hands, users quickly raise the questions of availability of more complete backfiles, more databases, simultaneous access, remote access, document ordering, and document delivery.

Networked CD-ROM system solutions are beginning to appear in the marketplace, with hardware and software available to allow simultaneous access to the same CD-ROM disk by multiple users. While such systems have their benefits, the networks are still limited to small numbers of users, with most supporting less than ten user site connections. More importantly, the CD-based systems are generating a demand for systems that offer the benefits of access to data over broadband networks to hundreds of simultaneous users.

Political and Management Considerations

While there is currently interest from many market segments in putting bibliographic information up in networked form, it comes at a time when much within the network community is in transition. That transition means that decision-making is often divided, conflicting technical information is frequently offered, and database issues can easily become clouded in the general politics of system growth and administrative control. Like any other transition, this one can provide opportunities, but database producers must not assume that their needs will be met without intense and continued involvement on their part.

Meeting the Demand

The demand for networked access to information can be met in diverse ways. Traditional network access to A&I services can and does provide at least a partial solution to many of the users' access needs. Yet, in other ways, the traditional means fall short when juxtaposed with the opportunities afforded by newer technologies.

The following section offers overviews of the types of technologically advanced networks and network communities being considered. Then, a historical look at some of the networked solutions long provided by the information community is taken, and some of the challenges those systems will meet in the 90s is discussed.

What's in a Network? It's Not Hardware and Media. It's Information and Users

A closer look can be taken at the number and types of networking options available and at the information environments of the people who use them. There are many aspects of networked information distribution that can be discussed independently of the type of network involved--factors such as the demographic characteristics of the user community, its work environment, and its information seeking habits. All of these factors play important roles in determining the systems and services that are to be designed. Rather than looking at networks and users separately, both will be reviewed together.

Types of Networked Systems

The two basic network types dealt with here are: telephone access networks of both the time-sharing and leased line types, and hard-wired systems, involving terminals and/or computers on local or wide area networks.

Dial Access Systems and Their Users

Dial or telephone access systems are designed to allow those with terminals or computers to use standard telephone lines to establish a connection to desired files. The telephone connection is generally through a time-sharing packet-switched network. For users with consistent, high volume usage, dedicated telephone lines to vendors can be leased.

The dial access connection can be a direct connection to an online vendor or host. It can also be a gateway connection, with requests mediated to varying degrees in the process of being passed on to other vendor(s) or host(s).

Direct connections involve the use of a mainframe computer and an interface supplied and supported by the vendor. This interface is generally command-driven direct to the mainframe retrieval system or intermediate system, also resident on the mainframe, to provide a more novice approach. In some cases, a micro-computer-based interface is also available, produced either by the vendor or other firms, to mediate further the search and retrieval process. Contractual arrangements are established directly between the vendor and the user.

Gateways can also take a number of forms. The simplest are those that pass requests from one host to another. The initial host, usually as a service to its users and a boost to its appeal as a "single source solution," arranges for access through its system to another host or hosts. In this case, the user is generally responsible for establishing

65

accounts with all host systems. At the other extreme are the gateways that provide an interface to the user, processing the information request and selecting the host, the files, the mode of access, and the charging systems that are to apply.

Gateways are gaining in popularity, and some files are available through multiple direct access and gateway systems. The goal is to have files available on or through the system that is the most familiar to users because the system that is easy and familiar for users is the one that is most likely to generate traffic on any given file. Gateways, however, have the disadvantage of moving the database producer farther from the users.

Dial access system users can be described in ways that will be useful for future discussion. The users tend to represent a more diverse community than their hard-wired counterparts. This heterogeneity stems from the fact that the dial access mode is a more practical one to address diverse information needs. Users' needs tend to cut across subjects and data types and to change over time. Many libraries fall in this heterogeneous category because they serve a diverse user community. Other users can be members of communities not large enough or unified enough to justify a system of their own. Dial access user communities are, therefore, large and scattered.

The telephone access systems designed to support such users display characteristics that are consistent with the overall usage patterns. Vendors group data by type--all bibliographic, for example--then, within that framework, try to amass a sufficiently large group of files to answer the varied questions that will be put to the system. In general, vendors operate on "the bigger the better" philosophy, so that a user can learn a limited number of systems and have access to a broad range of information within the information system.

Because of their sporadic and disparate usage patterns, dial access users can be hard for database producers to identify. Vendors do not usually report user identities to database producers. Gateway providers do not identify their users to the eventual host vendor. Users, themselves, rarely approach the producer directly.

Dial access users are also difficult to target, again due to lack of information as to who they are as well as the fact that their needs change. Usage can be controlled (i.e., such practices as differential usage fees for subscribers to paper indexes or members of certain societies, etc.) only insofar as the systems require account identification of some kind; but, again, individual users can enter systems under a variety of guises, the most common of which is simply the organization for which they work.

User skill levels can vary from the curiosity users who dial in at midnight, just to see what the system does, to the research scientists, trained in online searching. Often there will be a single person or, at best, only a few people within an organization who have been trained in system use. Again, the library serves as a good model.

66

Few assumptions can be made about the support that is available to users, including hardware and database support. Often there is little. Use of computer equipment of any sort may be new to users, and they can have no knowledge whatsoever of the basic functioning of a database or of the contents of a file.

In sum, dial access users can be a difficult group to target, to please, and to service. They are, however, a group whose collective usage patterns are well known to the information community and who are prime candidates for migration to networked systems when they are available on a broad distribution basis. When that time arrives, the dial access users are more likely to act like, and need to be treated like, their current hard-wired counterparts.

Hard-Wired Systems and Their Users

Hard-wired systems have their components permanently connected to network sources, as the name suggests. Access is available to those who are part of the authorized user group for the system. Examples include both local area networks (LANs) and wide area networks (WANs). Either terminals or computers can serve as access devices. The services offered on hard-wired networks depend on the capabilities of the host and the access devices. Hard-wired network services can include the option of access to remote or dial access systems as well.

Hard-wired system users can be characterized in several ways. These users tend to belong to a closed or at least closely defined user community: employees of a company, students and faculty at a university, etc. Usage can be controlled, for example, by seniority or status. Charging can be centralized, with the corporate sponsor paying licensing fees and the services then being provided "free" to qualified users. Users are known, or can at least be identified, on an individual basis.

Systems to track usage can be put into place. Indeed, such tracking systems tend to be in place already to provide traffic information to the network administrators. Additional post-system usage can be determined or sampled by producers via direct contact with the users.

Users of hard-wired systems tend to share common goals and have similar schedules. They may even have common subject backgrounds and similar training in system usage. Such users often have access to trained staff onsite for questions regarding network operation and database content.

Terminals form an integral part of users' work patterns in the hard-wired configuration. Terminals or workstations are at the users' desks; workstations stay connected all day, and often all night, and are used for everything from electronic mail to sophisticated data analysis and modeling.

Hard-wired systems also tend to have a variety of files and services available, grouped around subject or project criteria rather than around technology or file type. A university will have, for example, numeric data files, bibliographic files, and analytic programs that reflect the subject research interests of the academic community. The files that are available are heavily used, and they are used by a large proportion of the authorized community.

The diversity in the types of data available, the frequency with which the system is used, and the basic commitment to network use within the user community have important implications for the database producer. Equally important is the fact that these aspects of system usage are new to the information community, yet they will be the ones that more closely match the characteristics of future networks.

Information Providers as Network Suppliers

Remote distribution of bibliographic information is not new to most secondary information publishers. They have been providing A&I data for network distribution for decades. As noted above, however, there are many new aspects to the type of system and the type of users that are being served.

Historical Look at Network Distribution

Bibliographic databases have been available in a variety of networked and networkable forms for many years. The traditional form of implementation to date has been installation on a dial access vendor service. In general, such installation meant the use of outside vendors, such as DIALOG, or ORBIT and BRS (now both Maxwell Online systems).

The vendors signed contracts with database producers and provided centralized dial access systems to search the files of many producers. Earlier contracts often gave files on an exclusive basis to a single vendor. (These exclusives are now giving way to broader based, non-exclusive contracts.) Vendors converted files to a proprietary format, devised by the vendor, and mounted the files in magnetic form on a limited number of mainframe computers. Access was provided on a time-sharing basis over packet-switched networks.

Users were charged a fee based on connect hour time and citations printed or ordered as an offline print service. The vendor billed users for both the database usage and the telecommunications charges and returned a royalty payment and summary data on file usage to the database producer. The vendors also provided customer support services including system and file documentation, system training, and toll-free customer service.

In a few cases, systems were developed "in-house" by database producers, using licensed or original software. Dial access systems like this--STN and WilsonLine serve as examples--could be tailored to showcase and market a particular database family. They also offered an opportunity to retain contact with the user base and to trade off the costs of system maintenance and support with increased revenue. As online usage grew, however, users tended to want the smaller systems to grow to accommodate other files of particular interest to their needs. Thus, although these systems began as stand-alone vendors, they gradually became multi-producer vendors or at least gateways to other systems and files.

Some of the database vendors also offered their software for installation on customer mainframes; database vendors essentially became software vendors in this scenario. The customer was then free to contract for database services directly with the information producer. This option was selected by those customers whose usage volume or security needs justified it and/or who had extensive in-house files to maintain. Customers for such services tended to be pharmaceutical companies, oil companies, chemical research organizations, and government agencies. The customer signed license agreements with both the database producer(s) and the vendor. The database producer then supplied magnetic tapes to the vendor's software customer.

This type of system had several advantages for the database producer. There was usually little additional work for the producer beyond the development of a licensing fee structure. There was no change in format or frequency for the database tapes. The software vendor bore the primary responsibility for installing systems. The customer was responsible for ongoing operation and support. In addition, the database producer was in direct contact with its major customers. This local information model has continued and is in use today at many corporate sites and on various networked campuses. The 1990 Cuadra/Elsevier *Directory of Portable Databases* lists over one hundred databases currently available for licensing for in-house use.

Systems of the 90s--Similarities and Differences

For many secondary information providers, the basic production of networked files has changed little over the past few decades. Information providers have been producing files to send to multiple online vendor services and to direct license customers. Producers have learned (or sometimes been taught) the value of carefully written file specifications. They know how to link tape production to in-house acquisition and indexing operations.

Producers also recognize that even the specter of "reloading the file" on a vendor system to support new fields and features can be survived. The same tapes sent to the online vendors, along with complete technical specification, can usually be sent to a variety of other network applications, with the responsibility for converting and mounting the tapes falling on the host site.

What, then, do current network options offer in terms of challenges and rewards? In some ways, systems today differ little from their predecessors. In many respects, the licensing of databases for installation on a local CPU or file server for use in a multi-user, dial access environment is the very model being reincarnated today by both CD-ROM and networked access systems.

There are, however, some important differences in the proposed systems. These differences include:

The types and formats of data being requested.

The number and types of sites that are now able to offer "local" networked services.

The availability of internet networks to share files between CPUs and servers.

The traffic capabilities of networks.

The number of terminal types connected to networked systems.

The size, skill levels, and expectations of the users.

Data Types and Formats

Systems in use for the last twenty years distributed primarily bibliographic data. Today, there is increasing demand for full text and images. There are, to date, few systems that can handle text and images effectively, although many systems seriously plan to offer text and image access in the future. In the interim, there are several technical and some major contractual barriers to overcome.

Provision of A&I data in machine readable form is clearly not a problem for most publishers. Provision of the accompanying full text, although more common than a decade ago, is still often a major hurdle. Fairly structured data and text produced from highly automated systems are the types that can be most easily mounted on networked systems. Thus, directories, case law, statutes, business statistics, and newspapers are the types of full text most frequently available today.

Text from many other sources, such as textbooks, journal articles, fiction, etc., is not available. The text either needs to be converted into electronic form, is available in only an electronic publication format, or is held back by a publisher reluctant to release it in a networked environment in which use, re-use, and remuneration issues are yet to be resolved.

Conversion costs of full text from paper or microfilm are still generally high, and markets are still small. Materials must be rekeyed or scanned using optical character recognition (OCR) techniques. Although both keying and scanning techniques have shown reduced costs and increased accuracy rates in the last decade, either represents a substantial investment.

Images create yet another challenge in terms of conversion, storage, and transmission. Images are expensive to convert to digital form. Where images are needed, their quality usually must be high, requiring scanning at high resolution. Three hundred dots per inch (300 DPI) is considered a minimum, and even black and white images can easily take up a megabyte of storage at 300 DPI. Various compression schemes are available, and they help; but typical compressed sizes also run 100K. In both CD-ROM and networked systems, the large storage required by scanning (and compression) means that transmission of images can cause delays and transmission of entire articles or book chapters in image form degrades system performance and response time for all system users.

Proposed networks with broad band width, high capacity, fiber optic lines will be better suited to handle images. Although few of these networks are fully operational today, many are in the planning and prototype stages. In fact, there are important prototype systems in the early operational or planning stages. Several of them are discussed briefly in the Application sampler that follows (*see* p.74).

Investments in full text and image conversion are made even riskier in the face of unknown markets, although much of the current impetus for conversion is coming from users, not publishers. While the market driven nature of such input can provide some indication of a market for the products, users often have little understanding of the inherent costs, and expect lower prices than are now possible. On the other hand, publishers are hesitant to release text products with little or no control over their use.

Publishers are also being urged to produce their text in structurally tagged formats using generic systems such as Standard Generalized Markup Language (SGML) (*see* Chapter 2, p. 38). Such tagging systems are designed to increase publication and republication options by reducing conversion costs. The barrier is the fact that the up-front costs for retooling publishing operations are high. Although the potential return is also high, the payoff is in the future, not now.

There are still relatively few production or product applications that make full use of the tagging. There are, however, many such production and application support systems in the design and prototype stages, and their numbers are growing daily. Tagging is yet another threshold to be crossed in the 90s.

Pricing models, indeed, economic models do not exist. The base businesses that provide the products for the established market--oftentimes print, sometimes microfilm and/or online--must be able to exist through yet another format transition, and the routes through that mire are anything but charted.

Configurations

Current system configurations on which attempts are being made to construct networked systems vary greatly. The constraints of each system type bear a direct impact on product design, making product planning exceedingly difficult. Configurations vary from minicomputer networks at small universities and technical schools to multinational gateways.

The small schools want to mount a few, heavily used files in a networked environment. They may want more but can afford only a few. The schools want to put these few files up on a campus system or to network a limited number of CD-ROM workstations for access to the files by a large number of users.

The multinational gateways want to add additional bibliographic databases to their already vast offerings, either to attract new customer bases or to offer new services to hold existing customers already familiar with the gateway access routines and interfaces. If systems are connected to internet networks, on which files can be shared across networks and across platforms, the traffic problems become even more apparent. Most network applications consist of short bursts of data and transaction information being passed back and forth. The system transmits information quickly; the pauses are at the user's end, as the user deliberates his/her next move. Text and image retrieval systems must change that model to provide for transfer of large files on an interactive basis.

A common problem is the attempt by a network to support a wide assortment of installed equipment, ranging from "dumb" terminals to sophisticated workstations. In such cases, there are many compromises to be made in production and delivery. Products can be designed to support a range of platforms, but this support implies compromise.

Image display is a good example. Systems designed to display full page 300 DPI images on a VGA or Super VGA monitor can be configured to display them also on CGA level monitors. The CGA system will, however, need to have a system for panning and zooming the images in order to be able to see the entire page at a readable display resolution. Systems designed to print text images on a laser printer can also be designed to produce text output on a dot-matrix printer, but image print output is then lost.

While the challenges that such a range of installations present can be reduced to several major issues, the solutions fall quickly into many combinations and permutations. A look at some current products will illustrate some of these network interactions.

Primary and Secondary Publication

Much of the current planning and prototype activity is with full text documents. Partially, this is an historical consequence. Early development funding of network systems grew out of broader systems of support for research. As such, textual information on research work-in-progress became one of the primary types of data involved. The ability to exchange pre-published papers and reports generated a demand for the availability of published materials. The technical and contractual complexities involved in the delivery of published full text materials have slowed the implementation of such systems. While secondary services have long been providing networked access, such access is no longer enough for many users. They want the full text as well as images.

In order for full text search and delivery systems to operate in conjunction with A&I systems, there needs to be close cooperation between primary and secondary publishers. Each player must understand the history, constraints, goals, and time frames of the other.

Automated Alternatives

Keying operations, optical character recognition systems, and systems to generate structurally tagged text are becoming more widely available. Files of ASCII full text are often part of the data conversion for CD-ROM products, or they form the backbone for database publishing operations.

Once the text is available in machine readable form, it is a simple process to invert it as an "index" to the original text. If the input text is structurally tagged, so much the better; algorithms can be devised to select the fields to be used for indexing. A publisher could choose, for example, to include only title and chapter heading fields to build an index. This ability to use selected fields yields a smaller index but, hopefully, a richer one.

In any case, the resultant inverted full text is perceived by some as being a simple, obvious, and adequate solution to access needs. Most secondary database producers still, however, depend on the traditional labor-intensive method of using skilled human indexers to produce indexes and abstracts.

A key concern, therefore, is an understanding of the relationship between manual and automated "index" approaches. To simplify this discussion, the process of finding relevant information can be divided into two conceptual steps: first, the identification of documents likely to contain relevant information; and, second, the search within the identified documents for the occurrence(s) of the desired information.

Secondary indexes are specifically designed to perform the first step, the identification of likely documents. Secondary indexes use various techniques to facilitate this process: controlled indexing vocabularies, hierarchical vocabularies, field designators, use of human indexers with subject backgrounds, etc.

Inverted full text can, on the other hand, provide the advantage of searching across groups of documents and searching text in its entirety. It lacks, however, the control to group like concepts under identical vocabulary or to differentiate in-depth treatment of a topic from mere mention of or reference to the terms, etc. Inverted full text indexing serves, therefore, as a useful supplement and complement to secondary access rather than as a replacement for it.

The two access methods have had few opportunities to work together. Several CD-ROM based systems do allow access to secondary and primary information within the same system. For most users, this concept is new enough to be confusing at first. Once mastered, however, the ability to use both levels of indexing together offers many rewards. As storage and access capabilities increase, there will be less need to choose between the access systems to be used.

Application Sampler

Many pioneering systems are in the prototype and planning stages as we enter the 90s. Useful experience is being gained through their use. Conversion and tagging systems, product layouts and designs, retrieval systems and interfaces are being challenged and honed.

Current conversion products and prototypes using machine readable full text on CD-ROM are often in-house (e.g., training manuals, product documentation) or public domain (e.g., government publications, older materials) items. Yet, such projects bear watching; they are providing usage and system data that are sorely needed if the networked delivery of bibliographic and full text data is to become a reality. A few systems are briefly outlined below, to offer an introduction to the range of applications and producers involved.

Colorado Alliance of Research Libraries (CARL)

The Colorado Alliance of Research Libraries (CARL), a consortium of eight large research libraries in Colorado and Wyoming, offers its members and, through them, the general public access to various types of information via networks.

The CARL service includes:

> Catalogs of over 30 CARL libraries, including public, university, college and community college, and health sciences libraries.

> UnCover, a CARL generated (keyed) file of over 10,000 journals currently received by member libraries; table of contents information, including title and author(s), is searchable.

> Several Information Access Company (IAC) bibliographic databases available for searching as well as several IAC full text databases.

> Document delivery via the IAC full text files as well as fax from the CARL member libraries.

> Various information databases, including an encyclopedia, a local metropolitan information database, a book review database, etc.

Access is possible using a telephone and modem; a broad range of terminals and micro-computers are supported. Access is also provided through Internet. Local phone charges are paid by the patron, but there are no access charges for most services. A few of the databases are password-protected but are available to any patron with a valid library card from any of the participating libraries. There are charges for fax delivery or down-loading of articles, but the system accepts major credit cards.

Searching is simple, following menu prompts or using brief "quick" commands, if preferred. Library catalog records show holdings information from member libraries and circulation status. Searching in library reference rooms and from home computer terminals is essentially the same. Fax service is prompt and of good quality.

The CARL system represents an operational system being run in a real life environment, but it provides opportunities for experimentation and development as well. The member libraries rely on CARL to provide free patron access to their catalogs on a day-to-day basis. Yet, the system also affords a controlled and monitored environment in which to test user acceptance of full text, for-fee services.

EasyNet

EasyNet is a gateway system to over 900 databases. The system's goal is to allow users untrained on a variety of systems to make effective use of multiple online systems. This process is accomplished through a menu interface that prompts users to input their information needs. The EasyNet system then automatically selects the appropriate vendor and database for the search, formulates and executes the search, and returns the results to the user for review. There is also an advanced user interface option that allows the user to select the database to be searched directly.

Users are charged a flat rate per search. Contractual relationships are between user and network, between EasyNet and a variety of networks, and between EasyNet and the online vendors. Database producers do not receive direct information on who the end user is. EasyNet usage is an unidentified part of the connect hour data across accounts provided to the database producer by the online vendor.

In sum, the EasyNet system provides revenue to the database producer from users in a broad customer base. The user need not be responsible for the choice of database or database vendor, and the database producer does not know the identity of the user.

Stevens Institute of Technology

At Stevens Institute of Technology in New Jersey, all undergraduates are required to have personal computers. Stevens mounted a database of texts to support a class on Galileo and the Scientific Revolution. Students were expected to buy some of the texts, and the rest were available on reserve. Studies were made of usage patterns, and the results compared for student work. Although usage differed, general results showed an increase in the quality of the students' work. The database was micro-computer based but could easily be ported to run in networked environments.

Files such as the one at Stevens present a good example of the use of an already published text in a context in which the value of the text is increased by the ability to search it. In addition, the educational environment provides opportunities for controlling the user group being granted access, for monitoring actual use, and for analysis and control of re-use.

Oxford Dictionary of Quotations

The *Oxford Dictionary of Quotations,* produced by Oxford University Press, is now available online. The database contains 14,000 quotations from 650 authors and speakers. Each record contains the quote, the author's name, birth and death dates, quote source, and occasionally an explanatory note. It costs $60 per connect hour, $.20 per full record printed online, and $.50 per offline print.

The quotations file offers the ability to search on all the above fields, thus allowing the user to find topical quotes, to group quotes by a given author or speaker, or to complete or verify partially known quotes. In short, the dictionary provides the types of access that users have long wanted but were not able to have with a traditional paper product, no matter how well indexed. The quotation file represents a good example of the type of information that could generate use in a networked environment but that creates many rights issues if the retrieved text is to be incorporated into a speech or a text for publication.

NCSU and NAL Image Transmission Project

North Carolina State University (NCSU) Libraries, the NCSU Computing Center, and the National Agricultural Library (NAL) are collaborating in an ongoing research and demonstration project to discover and explore the issues involved in an NSFNet/Internet-based document delivery system for library materials. Scanned images of documents will be transmitted via the NSFNet/Internet computers for delivery to libraries, offices, and research stations.

The project is adhering to standards for data formats and communication protocols in order to integrate dissimilar computing environments in multiple locations. Full scale implementation testing is scheduled for 1990-1992. Copyright issues are being addressed in a number of ways, including the use of non-copyrighted materials and solicitation of rights from publishers. Research is also being conducted into the issues related to copyright as it pertains to transmission of digitized documents. Although the project does not have a secondary index component per se, it is expected to provide much needed experience and bring research resources to bear on the development of document delivery systems to support A&I system retrieval.

The above examples represent only a few of the possibilities for integration of secondary literature into networked environments. Many others are in the planning stages. The prime factor that will make such systems a reality is the development and implementation of proposed national network systems.

The next section presents several national initiatives that are of vital interest to the publishing community.

NREN

The National Research and Education Network (NREN) is a proposed high speed computer network to link universities, national laboratories, non-profit research organizations, and private companies engaged in government-supported research and education. NREN would consolidate and build upon existing interconnected telecommunications networks.

The existing networks are currently known as the Internet, a conglomeration of smaller foreign, state, local, topical, private, government, and agency networks of which NSFNet is the largest part. NSFNet was created to facilitate access to supercomputer facilities. It is now composed of regional and mid-level networks.

NREN would, as a high speed computer network, tie together many major U.S. government, research, industry, and educational networks into a master library research and information infrastructure. As of this writing (October 1990), a compromise NREN bill has been passed in the Senate and is awaiting approval by the House. The ultimate goal of NREN is to keep the U.S. competitive in the global marketplace, and activities are being staged to consolidate and upgrade existing networks and aggressively develop newer high speed networks for the future.

In the long run, NREN extends the promise that interchange of information within, between, and among institutions will be far more powerful and commonplace than it is today. Certainly, the progress of the NREN bill bears watching by all involved in the production and dissemination of information. Nancy Melin Nelson, in a recent issue of *Information Today*, commenting on the library and information conferences during the first nine months of 1990, writes:

> "A conference goer of any persuasion, however, would be likely to find him/-herself in attendance at a session on NREN (National Research and Education Network). If, in years past, this and other library conferences have supported an unusual number of sessions devoted to the topic of CD-ROM, this year's favorite attraction was certainly networking, and specifically the NREN."

The immensity of the task encompassed by the NREN proposal has engendered the formation of various groups to address many of the research and policy activities that will be necessary to make NREN possible. Indeed, some of the groups predate the NREN proposals and are directly or indirectly responsible for its development to date. The following section introduces several of these groups that are of particular interest to secondary publishers; more detailed contact information appears at the end of the chapter.

Corporation for National Research Initiatives (NRI)

The Corporation for National Research Initiatives is a nonprofit research and development organization founded in 1986. It brings together representatives of industry, government, and education to participate in the research necessary to create a true national network. The NRI recently received funding from The National Science Foundation to oversee the research to set up experimental networks and to experiment with hardware and software technologies. Funding commitments have also been obtained from major corporations.

EDUCOM

EDUCOM is a non-profit membership organization of colleges, universities, and corporate "associates." EDUCOM was founded in 1964, with the express goal of promoting the rational and effective use of information technology in higher education. EDUCOM member institutions have some of the most advanced networked campuses in existence today. EDUCOM provides an active meetings, seminar, and publications program.

Each year, EDUCOM's Networking and Telecommunications Task Force (NTTF) sponsors a National Net Conference as a forum in which education, government, and industry can meet to prepare for the activities that will be part of the NREN. Publishers are important participants in the activities of the National Net Conferences.

CAUSE

CAUSE (formerly College and University Systems Exchange) is an association of member institutions, corporations, and agencies whose focus is the management of information technology in higher education. The mission of CAUSE is to promote more effective planning, management, and evaluation of computing and information technologies in colleges and universities and to promote the professional development of its members.

Association of Research Libraries (ARL)

The Association of Research Libraries is an association of major research libraries in the United States and Canada. The ARL Task Force on Telecommunications is charged with the examination and evaluation of the implications of NREN for research libraries.

Coalition for Networked Information (CNI)

ARL, CAUSE, and EDUCOM recently announced the founding of the Coalition for Networked Information. The Coalition's mission is to promote the creation of and access to information resources in networked environments in order to enrich scholarship and to enhance intellectual productivity. The Coalition will address many of the policy, licensing, and standards issues that will be raised by the NREN initiative.

Issues and Challenges for Database Producers

For the producer, the technical aspects of networking data can be minor concerns. Far more important and longer term decisions remain to be made in the areas of markets, protection of intellectual property, standards, interfaces, corporate reorganization, and pricing.

Markets

Databases are being used by increasingly large numbers of people who are not known to the database producer, which leaves the producers with little data on which to base future product and market decisions. In addition, the current buyer or contractor for tape services may understand little about the contents of the files.

The purchasers and the users are becoming more and more isolated from each other. Without a known user base at whom to direct training and sales information, providers are lacking important decision-making data in terms of both product features and pricing models.

User Populations

The user populations for networked data will continue to grow and, with the advent of the proposed national networks, increase by orders of magnitude over the next few decades. Those users will also shift from being the untrained, low-use types typified by today's dial access users and move toward being the experienced workstation users.

Even more important than the users' experience will be the increased understanding of the database structures and resultant ability to appreciate the content of available tools. Users will also be more accustomed to integrating data across applications and will demand that publishers, providers, and vendors assist in this process.

Use, Re-use, and Control

As networks grow and more demand is placed on network administrators to provide text and index files, the technical personnel trained in hardware and telecommunications skills are having to deal with intellectual property rights and other publishing issues --areas in which they have little or no experience or training.

If a database is available through a gateway or network, is there any way to know more about how the data are being used? Or, more importantly to some publishers, is there some way to know whether and how the data are being re-used.

The reality is that little is really known about the ways in which people are using or are going to use data in electronic form. In most cases, more is known about electronic usage than about print material and photocopier usage, but there is no way of knowing what users do with information once they have downloaded it from the original host system and have incorporated it into other applications.

Beyond mere tracking, however, is the fact that it is going to be many years before users, themselves, know how to utilize the data on these systems in the best way possible. They simply do not have experience in accessing and using bibliographic data in electronic form. They are not used to having data available for search and retrieval on a local and repetitive basis.

An example will illustrate this point. If users need information on topic X and Y, they would traditionally do or request a search, online or in paper indexes. The search would result in the users' receiving a stack of pages containing many bibliographic citations. These citations would be visually scanned for items of interest and titles selected for document retrieval. The rest of the bibliography might well be retained as "fall backs," if the originally selected documents are not available or prove to be irrelevant.

The documents are then obtained either from the library, from other local sources, or from interlibrary loan. In any case, document retrieval generally includes consulting some sort of location list or catalog. Once the documents are obtained, and it can be days or weeks later, they are read and/or filed. Perhaps they are photocopied to take home, to show to a colleague, or to put on reserve.

The users have been involved in a multi-step, usually multi-day process that would be too tedious and time-consuming to repeat; therefore, the incentive to repeat the process the next time the information is needed is low, while the inclination to retain the materials obtained is high. The costs of keeping the materials is often high as well. Space, time, and intellectual effort are involved in setting up and maintaining a system to keep the subsets thus collected.

With systems that allow easy access to not only the bibliographic citations but also the documents, the scenario can be very different. Just how such integrated systems will be configured and how they will be used are not yet known. Actual usage will determine future usage. There has not been anything before like the search and delivery opportunity that such an integrated system offers; it is difficult to assess what the long term effects will be.

Consider one possible scenario: A user sits down at a terminal, accesses a bibliographic database, identifies documents of interest, calls for them in electronic form, either image or ASCII, reads them on the screen, downloads them or orders faxes, if necessary. The process takes a matter of minutes, and the user has not had to move from his/her desk or office. If the data are needed again, the user can easily and simply call them back off of the central system; the user has no ongoing responsibilities to save or organize the downloaded data.

Systems exist that provide for retention of search strategies, retention of search results (generally keys to the documents), and assignment of "trail markers" allowing users to retrace a search journey without having to remember it. Systems also exist that allow users to make annotations to text that can then be printed off, with the text or separately.

How often and how well such systems and features are used depend on many factors. Certainly, the interest and skill level of the users in navigating files of bibliographic data are considerations. A more important consideration, however, is how useful and flexible the data are. If the bibliographic files are part of larger systems that allow transmission of citations for use in document ordering, incorporation into bibliographies and works in progress, etc., use will be much greater and usually more sophisticated.

Of course, a consideration of the data use and re-use brings the focus back to control issues. The more powerful the systems, the more reluctant information providers will be to have their data involved, lest there be opportunities for abuse. A central question becomes the ability of the network to monitor use and to report usage patterns back to database providers. Information is needed on types of requests, duration of use, intended use, actual re-use, user background, and classes of users.

Standards

An essential ingredient in networked systems is the use of standard communication protocols and data formats. There are literally hundreds of protocols in use worldwide to handle transmissions at various levels and between various types of equipment. For an overview and discussion of many of these protocols, including application examples, the reader is referred to the work of John Quarterman, *The Matrix, Computer Networks and Conferencing Systems Worldwide* (1990). Suffice it to say that, as with any data interchange process, the adherence to standards provides rewards in flexibility of system application design and larger customer bases (*see* Chapter 2, p. 38).

Some of the protocols that the reader will find in discussions of networked systems are:

> **TCP/IP Transfer Control Protocol/Internet Protocol**, is a widely used protocol with applications at various network levels. It provides for remote login, file transfer, and mail functions.

> **X.25** is an asynchronous data link protocol supporting medium speed communications in the 56 kilobyte/second range. It is employed in Open System Interconnection (OSI) applications.

T1, T3 are series of data transmission systems. T1 means transmission at the rate of 1.5 megabytes/second; T3 is at the rate of 45 megabytes/second. NSFNet is currently transmitting at T3 levels.

Z39.50 is an American National Standards Institute (ANSI) ratified protocol designed to handle client-server (machine to machine) interactions for the retrieval of bibliographic information. Many see its widespread adoption as the key to more powerful information resources.

TIFF, Tagged Image File Format, is a set of image file formats widely used today in systems utilizing digitized images.

Interfaces/File Structures

Today, a given database often has a variety of interfaces applied to it. Some interfaces are able to utilize all of the detail included in the file; others lose detail, searching power, and/or options but make the file available and usable to a broader range of users.

Will the interfaces be standardized? A likely guess is that they will not. For most systems, reasons rooted in their basic architecture dictate many system functions and their appearance to users. Most systems have a user base to whom the existing interface looks and feels familiar and who are anxious to have it remain so.

Aside from commercial and competitive reasons for interface differentiation, individual applications do not have to look alike, rather they need to do their jobs well. An interface that is designed for and works well with structured text-like bibliographic records and directory listings can rarely deal with the demands of a full text system--and, vice versa. With interfaces, if it works, it's right; if it's right, it works. That doesn't mean, however, that they all have to look alike.

There are other options, however, for standardizing data that are, in the long run, more important than the interface question. With emerging conventions for micro-computer based applications and with the increased use of application level systems and their conventions (Microsoft's Windows 3.0 serves as a good example), there is a gradual growth in similarity of basic functions. This development builds confidence in new users to allow them to move on and discover more advanced functions, even if the functions are particular to an application.

There are also ways to have standard data input that allow any variety of necessary interface formats. Standard tagging systems are one way. Use of standard retrieval engines with filtered interfaces between data and engine is another.

From the database producer's perspective, the goal is to be able to produce and support a limited number of output formats for distribution. For the most part, this is an industry-wide concern as well. Having to convert data from one "standard form" to another, each step of the way, limits the options for use while simultaneously creating delays and increasing costs.

Ownership

As many firms have discovered over the last decade, the question of ownership plays an important role for the contemporary database producer. Smaller firms are being acquired by larger firms and conglomerates. These publishing giants control steps in the publishing process from generation to primary, secondary, and redistribution publishing. For the database producer, being part of a larger group can bring the advantage of resources and visibility but can also mean a change in the basic structure and operating environment of the business. Such internal integration, market share, and resource availability make a profound difference in the database producer's ability to compete in a marketplace that is increasingly interested in integrated solutions.

Pricing

While most agree that networked access provides a value-added dimension to data, few can agree on what that is worth. Networked systems are not alone. CD-ROM, tape licensing, online, and print services are constantly reviewing pricing strategies as technologies and business opportunities change. Networked solutions offer yet another challenge in identifying units of measure for information use--time, number of items viewed, number printed, number of potential users, number of actual users, etc. Now, in addition to not knowing what to use as a unit of measure, publishers do not have a detailed understanding of how networked systems will be put to use on a day-to-day basis.

As is so often the case, various usage and pricing configurations work in various circumstances; and, as has happened with other forms of distribution, it will take a while for the most workable and equitable ones to emerge. An important issue for the 90s will be the building of pricing and tracking systems that are flexible enough to respond to a variety of pricing algorithms. Another even more important consideration will be the willingness of producers and consumers to consider and experiment with various systems to support the necessary evolution of usage patterns while providing equitable payments to the supplier.

Networked systems offer the distinct advantage over all past systems of being able to monitor themselves. Users are usually identified as individuals, not as corporate entities; system logs are kept of usage times; and intelligent workstations and network servers can maintain logs of system usage and summarize these data for analysis.

Although issues of privacy are clearly involved, it is at least possible to obtain the needed information, so often impossible in the past. Systems to analyze use without infringement of privacy issues and/or with the permission of the participants offer valuable opportunities to gather needed usage information. Indeed, networks present options for more rather than less control than in the past.

Summary

What, then, are the key network implications for the 90s? Networks imply a need to convert to yet another form of distribution--a highly automated and flexible one. The capability to support network distribution systems with production systems that were never designed to do so is another concern. In many cases, this scenario will necessitate the simultaneous conversion of in-house operations and distribution systems.

Other network implications for the 90s appear below.

A need to deal with evolving standards, markets, and pricing systems.

An opportunity to return to more direct contact with users.

The discovery that users are increasingly knowledgeable and demanding.

Recognition of an increasing need to integrate products and services on a subject- or project-oriented basis, rather than by subject or format, which implies the need to integrate delivery systems and platforms that will support widely disparate data types.

Continued concern over protection of intellectual property, with the addition of built-in monitoring devices and increased opportunities for use and re-use.

The development of new pricing structures to build a market and yet provide sufficient revenues to support base businesses.

A profound change in the way information is generated and distributed.

An opportunity to offer the kinds of information systems that users have wanted for a long time.

Ultimately, all those involved in networks in the 90s--including author, publisher, database producer, network supplier, system administrator, and user--will need to work together, and work very hard, to provide the necessary guidelines, the standards, and the environment in which to experiment with what will become the integrated systems of the next century.

References

ARL/CAUSE/EDUCOM Coalition for Networked Information. 1990. "Mission, Themes, and Strategies." Washington, D.C.

Arms, C., ed. 1988. "Campus Networking Strategies." *EDUCOM Strategies Series on Information Technology*. Bedford, MA: Digital Press.

Arms, C., ed. 1990. "Campus Strategies for Libraries and Electronic Information." *EDUCOM Strategies Series on Information Technology*. Bedford, MA: Digital Press.

Blair, D.C. 1990. *Language and Representation in Information Retrieval*. Amsterdam, The Netherlands: Elsevier Science Publishers, B.V.

Blair, D.C. and M.E. Maron. 1985. "An Evaluation of Retrieval Effectiveness for a Full-Text Document Retrieval System." *Communications of the ACM*. 28(3): 289-297.

Cleveland, H. 1989. "How Can 'Intellectual Property' be 'Protected?'" *Change*. May/June 1989: 10-11.

Connolly, F., S.W. Gilbert, and P. Lyman. 1990. Preprint. *A Bill of Rights for Electronic Citizens*. Washington, D.C.: Office of Technology Assessment.

Cuadra C., ed. 1990. *Directory of Portable Databases*, Volume 1. New York: Cuadra/-Elsevier, New York.

Fisher, F.D. 1989. "The Electronic Lumberyard and Builders' Rights. Technology, Copyrights, Patents, and Academe." *Change*. May/June 1989: 17-21.

Fortier, P.J. 1989. *Handbook of LAN Technology*. New York: McGraw-Hill.

Gilbert, S.W. and P. Lyman. 1989. "Intellectual Property in the Information Age." *Change*. May/June 1989: 23-28.

Hogan, T., ed. "NISO Annual Meeting Scheduled This Month." *Information Today*. September, 1990. 7(8): 48.

Levine, A. 1990. *Global Copyright Issues in the Secondary Information Industry*. Philadelphia: National Federation of Abstracting and Information Services.

Loupe, J. 1990. "National Research and Education Network; Overview and Summary." *Linking Researchers and Resources: The Emerging Information Infrastructure and the NREN Proposal, ARL Briefing Package*. Washington, D.C.: Association of Research Libraries.

Loupe, J. 1990. "Quick Guide; Players, Networks, Definitions, Standards." *Linking Researchers and Resources: The Emerging Information Infrastructure and the NREN Proposal, ARL Briefing Package*. Washington, D.C.: Association of Research Libraries.

Markoff, J. 1990. "Creating a Giant Computer Highway." *The New York Times*. September 2, 1990. 3: 1.

Nelson, M. 1990. "Think big: NISO Meets in New York City." *Information Today*. October, 1990. 7(9): 1, 29, 33.

Nelson, N.M. 1990. "Conferences, NREN, and OCLC." *Information Today*. September 1990. 7(8): 15-16.

North Carolina State University Libraries. 1990. Press release. "The North Carolina State University Libraries and the National Agricultural Library Joint Project on Transmission of Digitized Images: Improving Access to Agricultural Information."

O'Leary, M. 1990. "Online Quotes Spice Stuffy Speeches, Season Dreary Documents." *Information Today*. October 1990. 7(9): 12, 14.

Quarterman, J.S. 1990. *The Matrix: Computer Networks and Conferencing Systems Worldwide*. Bedford, MA: Digital Equipment Corporation.

Contact Information

ARL/CAUSE/EDUCOM Coalition for Networked Information, 1527 New Hampshire Ave. N.W., Washington, D.C. 20036. Phone 202/232-2466. Fax 202/462-7849. Paul Evan Peters, Director.

Association of Research Libraries, 1527 New Hampshire Avenue, N.W., Washington, D.C. 20036. Phone 202/232-2466. Fax 202/462-7849. Duane Webster, Executive Director.

CARL Systems, Inc., 777 Grant, Suite 306, Denver, CO 80203. Phone 303/861-5319, 303/938-9353. Fax 303/830-0103. Ward Shaw, Executive Director. Martha A. Whittaker, Contract Administrator, Market and Client Relations.

CAUSE, 4840 Pearl East Circle, Suite 302E, Boulder, CO 80301-2454. Phone 303/449-4430. Fax 303/440-0461. Jane Norman Ryland, President.

Corporation for National Research Initiatives, 1895 Preston White Drive, Suite 100, Reston, VA 22091. Phone 703/620-8990. Robert Kahn, President. Vincent Cerf, Vice President.

EasyNet, Telebase Systems, 763 West Lancaster Avenue, Bryn Mawr, PA 19010. Phone 215/526-2800. Fax 215/527-1056. Stephen M. Moss, Vice President, Marketing and Sales.

EDUCOM, 1112 16th Street N.W., # 600, Washington, D.C. 20036. Phone 202/-872-4200. Fax 202/872-4318. Kenneth M. King, President.

National Agricultural Library, 10301 Baltimore Boulevard, Beltsville, MD 20705. Phone 301/344-1383. Fax 301/344-5473. Pamela Q. J. Andre, Associate Director for Automation.

North Carolina State University. The Libraries, Box 7111, Raleigh, NC 27695-7111. Phone 919/737-2843. Fax (Director's Office) 919/737-3628. Susan K. Nutter, Director of Libraries. John E. Ulmschneider, Assistant Director for Library Systems.

Stevens Institute of Technology, Castle Point on Hudson, Hoboken, NJ 07030. Phone 201/420-5100. James E. McLellan, Professor.

4

Pricing, Marketing, Customer Support, and Legal Implications

With the advent of online information in the early 70s, publishers were awakened to the threat of media cannibalization. There was considerable fear that online access to data would seriously erode the subscriber--and revenue--base of the print counterparts. While time proved that such erosion was a valid concern, the amount of erosion was not as great as originally feared. Several factors inhibited the extent of erosion: online connect charges (perceived as high by users), the variety of search protocols among online vendors, and the fact that online access was, by and large, limited to experienced information specialists--end users still demanded and used the print.

By the early 80s, the market had stabilized, and most database producers had reached a level of equanimity in balancing their print and electronic products--but not for long. In the mid-80s, the information industry witnessed a proliferation of personal computers and increased computer literacy of the general public. The developments resulted in a rapidly growing market for electronic information. With the development of CD-ROM technology and increasingly user friendly software, the strength of earlier, inhibiting factors that had prevented radical migration from print to electronic media was and continues to be diluted.

In 1979, Chemical Abstracts Service reported print sales accounting for 80% of its revenue; by 1989, that figure had dropped to 46%.[1] Other producers are experiencing similar trends. According to an industry report, 1989 revenues in North America for commercially available, electronic information reached $8.6; by 1994, revenues are expected to reach $15.8 billion, at a compound annual growth rate of 13%.[2]

In order to remain competitive and maintain market share, information providers must consider distribution of their products in electronic form. Such distribution should not, however, be implemented without serious consideration of the issues that, depending on how they are addressed up front, will either ease the financial impact of product migration or result in a gradual loss of profit margin.

Issues that must be considered are: (1) pricing and its long term impact on profit margins; (2) positioning of each product medium (online, CD-ROM, diskette, tape, print) to the appropriate market (end user vs. librarian/information specialist); (3) customer support, which can have a significant impact on retaining customers; and (4) protection of intellectual property rights through thoughtful licensing and networking agreements. Clear understanding of these issues/implications will allow the information provider to develop a strategic plan for launching the future print/electronic product portfolio.

Pricing Strategies

A number of variables must be considered when developing the price of a given product: cost (including ongoing costs for support and delivery of updates); product features, benefits, and value as perceived by target market(s), the competition; and the distribution medium. The medium, in fact, should be included in the product feature category and weighed accordingly as a pricing factor,[3] because it often restricts the volume of data distributed, the ease of retrieval, the update frequency, the degree of data manipulation, and other product characteristics.

In the early days of online, many producers, knowing that the incremental cost of delivering data to the vendor was minimal compared to the total cost of creating the database and/or print product, priced the electronic medium unrealistically low, taking a cost-plus approach to pricing rather than a value-added approach. As a result, there were some cases in which new revenue from online usage did not adequately replace the revenue lost from cancelled print subscriptions. This error should not be repeated. It is essential in the multi-media environment today that information providers prepare for eventual migration among the various media through which they distribute their products. Pricing strategy must be developed accordingly.

Methodology

The first step in developing a pricing strategy is to ask a few basic questions. (*see* Figure 1.)

> What are the costs for creating the database--the raw information that is to be distributed through different media?

Pricing Factors

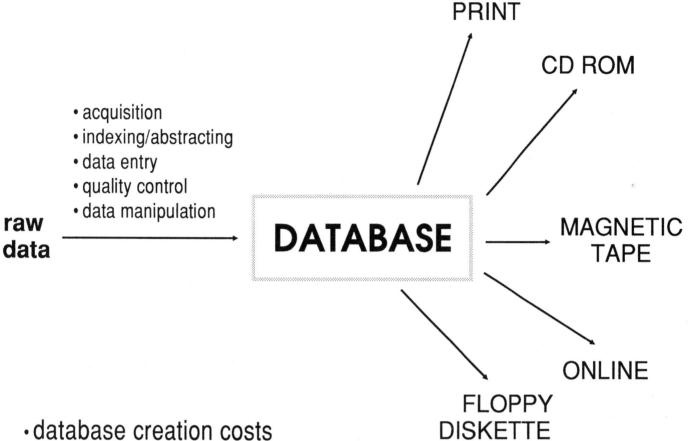

- database creation costs
- incremental production costs by media
- marketing/distribution costs
- overhead expenses
- potential audience
- competition
- product features/benefits
- potential usage
- product life cycle
- industry trends

-figure 1-

What medium will be utilized? What are the incremental costs of each?

What are the marketing and distribution costs?

What overhead expenses should be added?

What is the primary audience for each medium, and what are the purchasing characteristics of these audiences?

What is the competition in each of the markets, and how does the product in question compare--feature by feature--against the competition?

What is the competition charging?

What are the current stages in the life cycle of each medium?

What added value does each medium bring to the information being offered?

What are current and forecasted industry trends?

In most instances, the major costs or investments for any producer are in the creation and ongoing updating of the database from which information products are extracted. For long term financial stability, the cost of creating the database should be allocated to all products and not limited to the first one distributed, which is often the print version.

Consider the following scenario (*see* Figure 2). An information provider currently offers a print product. The database creation costs are $1,000,000 and printing/distribution costs are $500,000. With a subscriber base of 1,000, the unit cost (exclusive of sales/-marketing and overhead expenses) is $1,500. The producer then offers the product on CD-ROM. The incremental cost of distributing the data in this form is $200,000.

With an initial subscriber base of 200, the unit cost (exclusive of sales/marketing expenses, overheads, and database costs) is $1,000. (If the print product did not exist, however, the CD would have to bear the cost of creating the database, resulting in a unit cost of $6,000.)

Attracted by an artificially low unit cost, the producer could opt to price the electronic products lower than the print. This lower price, combined with the standard added benefits (quicker information retrieval, less storage space, use of boolean logic, etc.) of an electronic product, could create print migration to the point (for the sake of argument) where it was no longer cost-effective to produce the print. The subscription price for the smaller customer base would become prohibitive. The electronic product would then have to bear the database creation costs, and its price would have to be adjusted

Print vs. Electronic

"To allocate or not to allocate, that is the Question."

	<u>Print</u>	<u>Electronic</u>
Media Cost:	$500,000.	$200,000.
Database Cost:	$1,000,000.	——
Number Subs:	1,000	200
Unit Cost:	$1,500.	$1,000.
Media Costs:	——	$200,000.
Database Costs:	——	$1,000,000.
Number Subs:	——	200
Unit Costs:	——	$6,000.

-figure 2-

upward. (For an excellent case study on cost allocation among product media, *see Economies of Database Production* by Art Elias and Betty Unruh. NFAIS Report Series #1, 1991, p. 87.)

Granted, this scenario is not likely to bring dire results in the short term. A purely incremental cost-plus pricing strategy can, however, cause serious problems in the long term as subscribers shift from one medium to another. The customer is purchasing a commodity,[4] and that commodity is information, not the medium. The latter simply adds more or less value to the information being provided.

While a print product has higher incremental production costs than its electronic counterparts, from the producer's viewpoint, it has a minimal ongoing investment. From the users' viewpoint, it's easier to use and more portable than the electronic versions (*see* Figure 3).

The electronic products, particularly CD-ROM and diskette, have lower up-front production costs but higher ongoing support and R&D investments. To the users, these products offer greater search and retrieval capabilities than the print and allow easy, quick access to large amounts of data. It's true that "value" is subjective. When an information product is being sold to a specific market, however, the information provider must appreciate the value of the medium to the market; the medium must be priced accordingly.

Online Pricing Issues

Online was the first electronic distribution medium, starting in the early 70s. The online business is a well-established business. In the United States alone, there are currently 417 vendors offering more than 3,500 databases.[5] Pricing has long been an issue; but the industry standard--connect time charging--was set by Dick Kollin and Roger Summit in 1970[6] and endures today. With connect time charging, online searchers are charged for the length of time (number of connect hours) that they have logged on a database.

Early in the online life cycle, the concept of connect time charging was overlaid with a new set of fees called "hit charges." These charges were added for each item printed on- or offline and varied in cost by the amount of data received. In addition to connect hour fees and hit charges, the user also paid a telecommunications charge for the dial access. Since the early days of online, this pricing concept (connect hour fee, hit fee, telecommunications charge) has been employed. The pricing model can be predictable if search charges are estimated before the search is implemented and items are printed.

Issues by Medium

	Print	Online	CD-ROM	Diskette	Magnetic Tape
Provider Issues					
• Incremental Production Costs	HIGH	LOW	LOW	MEDIUM	LOW
• Incremental Production TIme	HIGH	LOW	MEDIUM	MEDIUM	LOW
• Ongoing Support	LOW	MEDIUM	HIGH	HIGH	LOW
• training					
• documentation					
• technical support					
• Frequency of Feature/Software Upgrades	LOW	LOW	MEDIUM	MED/HIGH	LOW
• R&D					
• upgrade packages					
Subscriber Issues					
• Capital Investment	—	LOW	MEDIUM	MEDIUM	HIGH
• hardware					
• software					
• Enhanced Search/Retrieval	—	MEDIUM	HIGH	MEDIUM	HIGH
• speed					
• complexity					
• Learning Curve	LOW	MEDIUM	HIGH	HIGH	MEDIUM
• software					
• hardware					
• features					
• Ongoing Ease of Use	HIGH	MEDIUM	MEDIUM	MEDIUM	MEDIUM
• Physical Storage Required	HIGH	—	LOW	LOW/MED	LOW
• Portability	HIGH	LOW	LOW	LOW	—

-figure 3-

97

Improved technology, new media, and other issues have brought the validity of connect time pricing into question.[7] In the 70s, for example, the most common transmission speed for data was 300 baud. Today, 1200 baud rates are fairly common; 2400 is becoming more accessible; and 9600 is predicted for the not-too-distant future. As a result, searchers receive much more information than before within the same time period, and searchers without access to high speed equipment are being penalized by the connect time pricing methodology.

In addition to the higher baud rate, connect time pricing has also been undermined by the existence of software packages that permit searchers to fine-tune their strategy before going online and that, in turn, allow them to download the search results so that browsing, manipulation, etc., can also be conducted offline. While such packages help to compensate (from the users' viewpoint) for the slow typist or slow search speed (due to heavy usage of the vendors' systems), they also have a negative impact on the information provider's revenue.

Experienced searchers, who encourage end users to search independently, strongly believe that connect time pricing is a major constraint to the development of a true end user market. Such pricing, they say, inhibits browsing and interactive "communication" with a database, while encouraging the speed of searching--get in and out as quickly (and cheaply) as possible.

So what is a fair pricing strategy? Certainly search speed--and the resultant revenues --bear absolutely no relationship to the value of the information being purchased, neither in quality or quantity. Is there a pricing structure that meets the current requirements of user, vendor, and provider? In recent years, new methodologies have been implemented. A few of these departures from traditional pricing are discussed in the following section.

Alternative Pricing

Chemical Abstracts Service

Effective January 1, 1988, Chemical Abstracts Service (CAS) moved from connect hour pricing to search term based fees. According to John Harry, Forecasting and Pricing Section, and Dick Kaser, Communication and Planning Department, at CAS, "Continuing use of connect time as the principal pricing component impedes further development of the online market because traditional connect hour pricing does not provide an economic incentive for database producers to enhance and develop their databases for optimal performance in an electronic environment."[8] The CAS objective was to place the value where it belonged--on the information retrieved. Charges were based on the search terms, themselves, as well as on each record extracted from the CAS file for use as a search term. A use charge was also added for each partial record used when browsing the search results.

CAS planned to reduce the connect time fee gradually; reductions took place in 1989 and, again, in 1990. CAS estimates that connect time charges in 1990 will be approximately 40% below the 1988 level when the new pricing methodology was introduced.[9] According to Jim Seals, Director of Marketing and Corporate Development, connect hour charges accounted for more than half of the CAS electronic revenues in 1979 but now amount to only about one-fourth.[10] Indeed, the new CAS metrics account for almost 60% of CAS electronic revenues (this includes charges for online displays which were not levied in 1979).

CAS new pricing strategy raised considerable controversy in the industry. Several vendors believed that they were given insufficient time to alter their accounting algorithms to accommodate the CAS metrics; as a result, they continued to use connect hour charging--simply passing on costs to the users until the appropriate changes could be made. The overall impact of the change is thus difficult to gauge. In any event, CAS action in this regard was significant. It brought into focus the multitude of debates on how to place appropriately real value on information. Whether CAS tactics prove ultimately to be successful in no way diminishes the fact that its objective is on target.

Mead Data Central

Over the years, Mead Data Central has attempted to minimize the overall impact of connect hour charges by introducing a level of pricing based on computer resources.[11] The major MEAD target is the legal market, which they entered in 1973 with LEXIS--a full text legal research service. Mead's pricing objective was to distribute the cost of searching equitably among all users--with heavier users bearing more of the burden.

Unfortunately, this pricing was extremely complicated and had to be changed to a scheme based on the kind and amount of data accessed. (NLM also implemented similar pricing in 1983. It was based on the computer effort required for a given search --and the amount of data retrieved--to establish equitable charges and place value on the information received.) The Mead charges vary by the file accessed, resources used in accessing the data (e.g., highly posted terms), online/offline printing, etc.

ESA-IRS

In January, 1989, ESA-IRS, a major European online host, changed its pricing structure to reflect "pricing for information."[12] According to Marino F. Saksida, Director of ESA-IRS, the objective was to charge for information retrieved and to eliminate connect hour pricing not simply reduce it as CAS had done.[13] To increase market size, the new pricing was to destroy the barriers to effective searching that connect hour pricing has raised in the eyes of the end users (the compulsion to get in and out quickly, limit interactive give and take with the database, etc.).

The pricing scheme is as follows. A "housekeeping" fee (about $12 U.S.) is charged when the user accesses the ESA-IRS computer. A session fee (about $6 U.S.) is added when the user accesses a database and enters a search command. A session fee includes unlimited access to the database--search time is not a constraint. Hit display charges have been established that are, however, higher than in the past; the basis for these charges is in alignment with charging for information.

According to Saksida, the results to date show that users are responding to the decreased pressure with regard to the time they spend searching. While ESA-IRS business has only increased 10%, users are staying online longer and performing longer searches. Preliminary user response has been favorable.[14] Users feel liberated from time constraints and freer to test new databases and try new, creative search techniques. Only time will tell whether the initial response will continue and whether the pricing will attract new users. Very few U.S. searchers access ESA-IRS (less than 1% of the overall subscriber base), chiefly due to the telecommunications charges incurred in transatlantic transmissions.

Telebase

Telebase Systems in Bryn Mawr, PA provides an end user-oriented system (EasyNet) with flat-fee pricing. The EasyNet system, established in 1984, has been praised as a revolutionary approach to true end-user searching, and it has been continually improved.[15] For approximately $10, the user is allowed up to ten hits for a single search. Another fee of $10 is added for each additional increment of one to ten hits for a single search. This pricing scheme is under evaluation and may be modified in 1991.

Telebase, itself, produces/owns no data; it is a gateway to other vendor systems with which it has negotiated large volume discounts. Telebase pays the telecommunications charges and encourages users who initially receive no hits to call the Telebase help desk and try again.

The pricing structure appeals to end users with little or no search experience--it's simple, seemingly inexpensive, and free of time constraints. Whether such pricing will reach its ultimate objective of breaking open the end user market for Telebase remains to be seen.

Fixed Rate Pricing

A variation on the Telebase pricing strategy that vendors and information producers are seriously considering is charging a fixed/flat rate for unlimited access to data. This strategy, however, is a complex. It must consider a series of factors: the number of users, the type of user, the amount of data retrieved, as well as the eventual revenue impact on all the other distribution media through which the same data are disseminated.

Needless to say, fixed rate pricing is not widespread. While this strategy possesses the distinct advantage (familiar to providers of subscription products) of guaranteeing up-front revenue that will be received before the product is "shipped" (unlike the established "pay-as-you go" approach of online usage), significant thought must go into the development of such a strategy. Flat rate pricing for online is analogous to licensing data on magnetic tape or selling data on a CD-ROM, but usage via these media is usually tightly controlled by license agreements that govern networking, downloading, re-use of the data, the number of sites that can access the data, type of access (interactive, batch SDI), among other concerns. In addition, these controls are usually agreed to directly by the users.

It is fair to say that as more organizations want access to large databases without incurring the hardware/software/support costs incumbent in running a local online system, fixed fee pricing arrangements will become more common. More than likely, these arrangements will necessitate trilateral agreements between the vendor, producer, and user to protect the rights and privileges of each party (*see* NFAIS Gateway Code of Practice for a summary of rights and privileges).

Future Trends

While connect hour pricing continues to be the standard, the winds of change have stirred. Pricing for information--preferably via a structure that is technology independent--is the current objective. According to Roger Summit, President of Dialog Information Services, the criteria for an adequate online pricing scheme are that it be understandable, controllable, and predictable by the user and that it relate to the value (or perceived value) of the information received.[16]

When a producer makes a file available online through a second party vendor, it will have to adopt, to a certain extent, the policies of that vendor. It is essential, therefore, that producers choose a vendor(s) with harmonious pricing philosophies. There are many pricing schemes in existence;[17] it is unlikely that uniformity among them will occur in the near future. Information pricing is complex. No one scheme will ever satisfy the needs of each party in the information retrieval chain. In the long term, a satisfactory pricing structure may be achieved with cooperation--and compromise--among the producers, vendors, and users, alike.

Magnetic Tape Pricing Issues

In the past six years, there has been an increasing demand from both corporations and universities to license databases for in-house use. This demand arises from a variety of factors--a decline in hardware/software costs, a desire to minimize telecommunication expenses, an increase in end user searching (no connect hours involved), and the perceived need to protect the confidentiality of searches.

There are two primary ways for the information provider to distribute the tapes: (1) directly to the customer and (2) via a program such as BRS OnSite and analogous services offered by NOTIS, IDI, and other software developers. The former method requires the producer to create and send the tape as frequently as contractually agreed upon as well as provide a level of support and training. The latter method eliminates the need to provide a tape to the subscriber and lessens (but does not completely eliminate) the issue of support. With BRS OnSite and analogous programs, the software provider distributes the tape and updates in the format required as part of a turnkey system (software/databases). The database provider, in return, pays the software vendor a percentage of the database license fee.

The norm is to license or lease data on magnetic tape rather than to sell it outright. The database provider thereby retains ownership/copyright of the data contained on the tapes, while the licensee or lessee is allowed to use the data within contractually agreed upon guidelines for a given time period.

Although the incremental costs attached to distributing magnetic tapes are real, they are insignificant when compared to other media. In determining costs, the sales effort (six months to close a deal is not an uncommon time frame, due to the contractual discussions and high level of investment on the subscriber's part), must not be ignored, nor the expenses of tape preparation and mailing, documentation and support. The major issues to consider in price setting are: kind of usage, number of and type of users, and the impact on revenue from other distribution media.

> **Usage:** Usage must be clearly defined and controlled; this is accomplished via the license or lease agreement. Issues that must be nailed down are: potential commercial use of the data (can they be resold?); creation of derivative databases; interactive versus batch searching; and copying of the tapes.

> **Users:** The user also must be clearly defined. Will users access the data at a single site or from several locations? Are the users to be affiliated with the organization licensing/leasing the data (e.g., students, faculty of a licensed university) or can anyone have access (e.g., users of a public library)?

> **Revenue Impact:** The provider should be aware of the potential revenue impact on its other products. Will the usage of the data on magnetic tape encourage use of other services, e.g., document delivery? Will it discourage/encourage use of print and other online products? Will multiple copy subscriptions be reduced? Any revenue loss is, in reality, a cost of distributing data on magnetic tape.

There are several pricing strategies that can be applied.

> **Pricing by number of sites** defines, in the license agreement, the number of physical locations that can access the data, e.g., the main campus of a university

and a number of specified satellite campuses. Pricing at this level, however, has serious pitfalls: (1) it does not take into account the real usage of the system; (2) sites can vary drastically in their user population (e.g., one lab can have hundreds of researchers while another site may have only a handful), which makes site pricing difficult to "sell" to small sites not wanting to pay the same high fee charged to larger sites; and (3) sites can be merged with resultant revenue loss.

Pricing by number of users is becoming the preferred approach. It establishes prices based upon the maximum number of users that can simultaneously access the database. This number is clearly specified in the contractual agreement, and wording is included to require usage reports and/or system audits. The major advantages are that the pricing is simple, predictable, and manageable for both the licensee and licensor, and it provides for revenue growth as the user base builds. In this case, there is certainly incentive for the producer to train and promote usage at the licensing organization, which, in turn, is a benefit to the licensee.

Pricing by margin is effectively a "let's protect the current business" approach. The producer calculates the potential revenue that would be gained from selling the data in other media (e.g., print/online) to the target audience and uses that number as a benchmark in establishing the license fee. If a consortium of universities, for example, wanted to license data for access by all members of the consortium, the provider would assess which current information products are sold to that group and are at risk. The sum of those potentially lost revenues would then be used as a starting point for developing the fee.

Future Trends

Interest in licensing data on magnetic tape is continuing to grow, particularly among academic consortia and within the large research industries (e.g., pharmaceutical, chemical). The major attraction is the fixed/flat pricing which encourages usage, especially to facilities with excess computer capacity.

Magnetic tapes accounted for 8% of electronic information revenues in 1989 ($687 million). Although this percentage is projected to decline to 5.6% in 1994, the estimated revenues at that time will be $866.5 million.[18] The tape licensing market remains a good source of incremental revenue for a relatively small investment. The investment is further reduced if the producer participates in an OnSite-like program with a software vendor that eliminates the cost of tape production/mailing and decreases the amount of support required.

CD-ROM Pricing Issues

CD-ROM is growing significantly as an information distribution medium. The number of products offered in this format has increased from zero in 1985 to an estimated 600 by year end 1990.[19] As mentioned earlier, the distribution medium is a feature of a product--it adds more or less value to the core information. CD-ROM has proven, in the few years since its inception, to be a medium feature that adds considerable value to a product from the users' point of view. It saves shelf-space, provides fixed fee access to large databases, allows for quicker and more complex searching than a print index, and eliminates telecommunication charges, and connect hour fees.

From the producers' point of view CD-ROM is an inexpensive distribution medium for databases that, in print format, equal large, multi-volume indexes. Unfortunately, because of the lower production cost, several producers initially priced their CD products low, hoping to capture market share. In reality, the producers captured only huge losses and learned a valuable lesson. Today, approximately 75% of CD titles now carry price tags that are more than twice those of the print equivalents.[20] (*see* Figure 4 for examples).

The producer that sets out to answer the questions recommended in the beginning of this chapter in order to develop a sound pricing strategy should also consider the following CD-ROM questions:

Are the CD product and the supporting software being developed by the producer or a second party; e.g., SilverPlatter? What is the cost differential between the two approaches?

How many CD players exist in the target markets to which the product is being sold? Will the product have to be "packaged" with hardware to speed market penetration?

Will the CD provide access to online files, thereby generating an additional revenue stream?

Will the CD have dial access from remote sites, possibly cannibalizing revenues from online and/or multiple CD sales?[21]

Can the CD product be networked within a site, and how will this possibility affect potential multiple sales (e.g., main library and department libraries within a university)?

Will the CD be distributed by the producer and/or a second party, and what are the resultant market implications?

Print vs. CD-ROM Price⁺*

	1990 Print	1990 CD-ROM	%
Biological Abstracts	$4,425	$7,660	73%
Science Citation Index	$8,850	$10,200	15%
Engineering Index	$1,685	$3,450	105%
Library & Information Science Abstracts	$445	$995	124%
Thomas Register	$240	$1,495	523%
Psychological Abstracts	$995	$3,995	302%

*Prices are institutional rates for the annual subscription. Discounts and print/CD combo rates are not included.

+ As published in Directory of Portable Databases, Cuadra/Elsevier, Vol. 2, No. 1, June 1990

-figure 4 -

CD-ROM pricing is essentially fixed fee pricing for unlimited, but controlled use; the controls are set in place by the license agreement. CD pricing strategies are identical to those applied to the magnetic tape medium. It should be noted that the classic online pricing model (connect time/hit charge) can be applied if a "meter" is built into the software (this approach applies more to networked CDs than stand-alone disks).[22] Such pricing will, however, negate one of the major perceived advantages of CDs--predictable, fixed fee pricing.

Future Trends

The phenomenon of CD-ROM is growing rapidly. In 1989, CDs accounted for 4.1% ($352.1 million) of electronic information revenue and are expected to rise to 14.1% ($2.88 billion) in 1994.[23] Future pricing trends are difficult to predict because of the relative youth of the medium.

Diskette Pricing Issues

Pricing issues for diskettes are analogous to those already described for CD-ROM. Additional concerns to be addressed are:

What types of PCs are in the target market(s) (e.g., IBM, MAC, NEC)?

What product formats should be offered (i.e., high density, low density, 5.25", 3.50")? Should the product be available in all formats?

What sales volume is expected? Would disk replication at this volume be more cost-effective conducted offsite or onsite via a facilities management program?

As with CD-ROM, diskette pricing is essentially a fixed-fee for unlimited usage, controlled by a license agreement.

Future Trends

The number of information products offered on diskette is beginning to increase rapidly. The first issue of the *Directory of Portable Databases*,[24] released in January, 1990, listed 66 diskette products; the second edition, issued only six months later, listed 223 diskette products.[25] In 1989, this medium accounted for 3.5% ($300.6 million) of electronic information revenues; it is expected to account for 3.2% ($506.6 million) in 1994.[26]

The diskette medium is somewhat limited by the storage capacity. (5.25" high density diskettes store 1.2 megabytes, whereas low density diskettes store considerably less). The provision of frequent updates, in which the updates consist of several diskettes, can be cost-prohibitive to the producer and annoying to the subscriber.

Other Issues For Consideration

Many information providers offer discounts. This option should be considered for inclusion in any pricing strategy, e.g., academic discounts, reduced rates for online searching at off-peak hours, reduced electronic product rates for print subscribers, bulk rates to single ship to addresses, multiple copy rates. It is worthwhile to review the competition's discount policies before entering a market with a new electronic product.

Marketing Issues

Electronic information products have a very large, aggregate potential market. Within that aggregate market are quite distinct groups, each with unique needs (and budgets), to which the products must be positioned differently.

Traditionally, electronic products (online) have been used by intermediaries (librarians, information specialists)--experienced searchers who can efficiently and cost effectively work with these products to retrieve the diverse information requested by their clients. More recently, with the addition of user friendly interfaces to online services and the increased computer literacy of the general public, intermediaries can more easily be bypassed. The data can be accessed directly by the requestor (*see* Figure 5). This trend substantiates the advent of what has come to be known as the "end user" market.

In the eleven years since the term, end user, first appeared in the literature, the market has grown but not as quickly as originally anticipated.[27] The increasing availability of CD-ROM and diskette media, however, has added fuel to the growth of the user population. While end users are not necessarily familiar with online searching--it is not within their daily routine[28]--they are familiar with PCs, diskettes, etc. and are becoming comfortable accessing information directly through using these tools. Such usage may eventually entice them to access the wider scope of data available online.

While the methods of selling information products to each of these markets (intermediary, end user) differ, they usually are clear cut in nature. Some sales processes such as licensing data on magnetic tape can be quite complex due to the number of players involved in the approval process, e.g., the information specialist, the data processing staff, and the end user who will ultimately access the information.

It is the rare electronic product that will appeal to equally to all three groups; priorities vary among hardware/software requirements, budget constraints, information needs, and the professional charter of each group. End users have only selfish needs to consider, while librarian/information specialists and data processing departments must satisfy the needs of a large and often diverse customer base. Relatively speaking, the latter two groups usually have more resources--financial and capital--than the end users.

DATA ACCESS

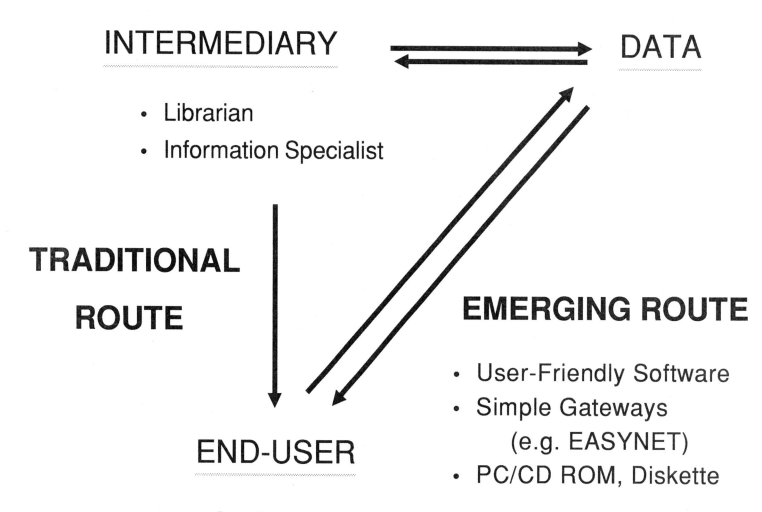

INTERMEDIARY → DATA

- Librarian
- Information Specialist

TRADITIONAL ROUTE

EMERGING ROUTE

- User-Friendly Software
- Simple Gateways (e.g. EASYNET)
- PC/CD ROM, Diskette

END-USER

- Student
- Faculty
- Researcher
- Professional
- Consumer

-figure 5-

It is essential that the information provider recognizes the key players in the purchase decision process and their individual concerns and objectives. It is also essential for the information provider to combine the information effectively with the electronic distribution media most appropriate for a given market (*see* Figure 6).

Large quantities of data (retrospective searching, cumulations, etc.) are better suited to online and CD-ROM distribution. In most disciplines, the primary market for these products will be the library or information center, even though the ultimate user of the data is someone else. Small portions of data can be cost effectively distributed directly to the end user on diskette or CD-ROM. Frequency of updating (if applicable) must also be added to the equation, e.g., it is usually more cost effective to distribute weekly updates of reasonable quantities of data on diskette rather than on CD-ROM. (Refer to Figure 3 for comparative production costs/time per medium.)

Assuming that the information resides on the appropriate electronic medium and that a product has been developed that satisfies a given market, what are the important sales issues?

Library/Information Center

For the majority of information providers, the library/information center has been the traditional marketplace for print and online products. The issues facing most libraries today are shrinking budgets and escalating periodical costs, primarily due to the currency exchange impact on foreign journals. According to a recent report,[29] academic research and medical libraries had the biggest spending increases while corporate and high tech libraries had the smallest. Budget expenditures for print (8% on average) continued to be higher than those for CD (6.35%) or online (6.04%).

Some libraries are implementing policies that require information to be purchased in one format only, e.g., print or CD--not both, in order to control expenditures. For most publishers, these policies imply that it will be difficult to maintain both a print and a CD-ROM subscription for a given product at a library without substantial discounting or promotion. Positioning electronic products within the traditional library environment will be an ever more challenging task!

Online

The librarian/information specialist (intermediary) has specific requirements: s/he must house and provide both current and retrospective data on a wide variety of subjects within specific budgetary limitations. Online access to data is viewed by the librarian as complementary to the limited number of books, journals, and reference tools that any library can reasonably afford to purchase.

109

DATA PACKAGING

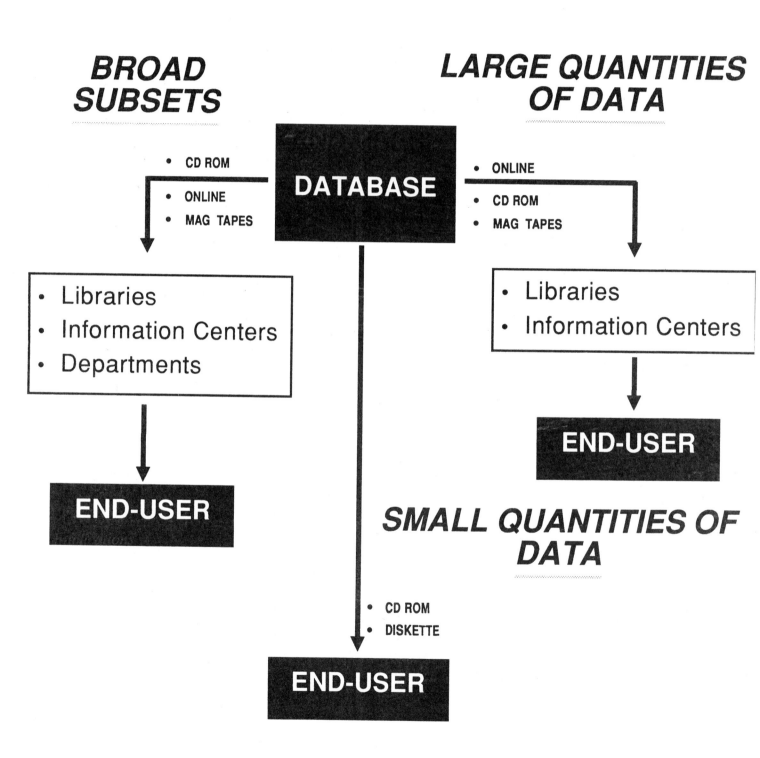

-figure 6-

A recent study[30] shows that both print and online services are necessary to the reference librarian. Online searches proved to be faster and more comprehensive in retrieving data on conceptual questions, while the print was faster in retrieving factual information. Although online vendors will promote online usage, database producers must take responsibility for promoting their individual files. Vendors can neither show favoritism towards any one file nor afford to promote extensively all files equally.

Within an academic or corporate setting, the librarian/information specialist is the key target for database promotion. This specialist is still the primary customer for scientific, technical, and professional online information. Not only will the librarian be performing searches as intermediary for the ultimate user of the data, but s/he will also be directing the more confident end users to appropriate databases.

The producers can promote usage of their databases to this key contact through:

Onsite training sessions (with online, selling equates to training and ongoing support through update sessions).

Participation in vendor training sessions.

Advertisements in vendor bulletins and newsletters.

Free posters (describing how to access the file, its features, etc.) that can be placed in the library and increase the visibility of the file.

Articles (by users) in library journals extolling the virtues of the database.

Press releases to announce new files/enhancements.

Exhibits and product reviews at major library meetings and online conventions.

Reduced connect hour rates for subscribers to the print version of the database.

User manuals, fact sheets, and sample searches that promote the unique features of the database.

Direct mail promotions to members of the special, medical and American Library associations.

Training files that can be accessed at low cost.

Discounted online or free time promotions for limited time periods to attract new users.

Promotions to library schools to ensure that future librarians are aware of the file.

Ongoing customer contact through site visits, telephone calls, and print and online newsletters.

The training and ongoing support for librarians/information specialists cannot be over-emphasized. These activities are critical to continued online revenue.

It is true that, when data available in printed form are also made available via online, print subscriptions will decline to a certain extent. The erosion will occur primarily among customers who were probably already considering cancelling the print due to limited product use and/or price sensitivity. Some database producers offer reduced online rates to print subscribers in order to maintain their print base. This practice works with organizations that exhibit heavy online usage.

CD-ROM

While online files certainly complete the reference librarian's portfolio of research tools, they also add considerable cost--the connect hour/hit charge/telecommunications scenario mentioned earlier. CD-ROM is now being viewed as a possible alternative to online searching in the library environment.[31] With CD-ROM, once the requisite hardware/software are in place, the ongoing cost of searching is minimal due to the elimination of the connect hour charges. The remaining cost is the purchase/license fee for the databases on CD-ROM. These fees vary considerably database by database, but it may be more cost effective for a library to acquire a heavily used file for virtually unlimited CD use rather than follow the traditional online pay as you go approach.

It is essential that information providers know the extent to which CD-ROM technology has been adopted in their target markets. The distribution of CDs by library type was recently reported.[32] (*see* Figure 7) Special libraries have not yet strongly supported CD-ROM; this trend may account for the stability in online revenues since the advent of CD-ROM technology. (It is predicted, however, that because special libraries have a much higher budget allocation to non print information, online revenues will shrink once at least half of these libraries adopt CD-ROM.)

The biggest hurdles to selling CD-ROM to the market are:

Availability of the requisite hardware/software.

Current transitional period in many libraries in regard to electronic service decisions (e.g., Is CD-ROM the answer? Should the library license tapes?).

CD'S BY LIBRARY TYPE

	CD'S		NO CD'S	
	U.S.	W. EUROPE	U.S.	W. EUROPE
ACADEMIC	57%	16%	43%	84%
PUBLIC	57%	7%	43%	93%
SPECIAL	18%	5%	82%	95%

-figure 7-

Networking requirements (e.g., Can the product be distributed via a local area network (LAN)?).

Legal issues (e.g., obtaining approval on the license agreement, solving networking issues, etc.).

Computer literacy in the target market.

Perceived value of the CD versus its print counterpart, versus competitive CD and print products.

These hurdles are not insurmountable, but they can slow down the overall sales process. Approaches that will help to minimize the impact of the above are:

Supply hardware, where cost effective. Do not, however, offer hardware maintenance; be sure that the hardware supplier manages equipment support.

Distribute the product via an established service in the desired market, e.g., SilverPlatter Information, Inc.; Dialog Information Services, Inc.; Cambridge Scientific Abstracts; etc. (If the provider has developed its own software and is directly distributing the CDs, the sales impact of distributing another CD version via outside organizations must be also considered. These organizations usually take a standard software approach to packaging all of the information that they distribute.)

Provide consultations to library customers; help them in identifying--and meeting --their technical needs. They will remember this service at purchase time.

Develop well written, logically structured user manuals, along with quick guides for easy reference to frequently executed commands.

Institute clear, straightforward networking policies, and make the license agreements as simple as possible while still protecting copyright. A cumbersome agreement can bog down the process.

Create demo diskettes that highlight the major features of the product.

Develop trial programs so that a library can use the product at no charge for a limited time (follow up with telemarketing and/or a direct sales call). Space ads will create product awareness, but it is the opportunity to use the product that closes the sale, particularly for those CDs perceived as being expensive.

Offer on-site training, if justified by the potential revenue stream.

Provide fact sheets that extol the features of the CD product and its complementary relationship to print and online.

Promote customer support services.

It is often the case that faculty/user recommendations influence the decision to add a new title to a collection. The majority of CD-ROM products, however, do not represent a new title to librarians but rather a new medium for a known entity. It is the features/benefits of the data in this format that must be sold--search speed, shelf-space savings, elimination of online charges, development of end user search capabilities, etc. Trial programs and sample diskettes, along with effective marketing material and direct follow up, work well in selling to the library market.

Diskette

Since the distribution of information on diskette is relatively new, trends are difficult to predict. The diskette medium, except where distributed over local area networks, has not been tremendously successful in the library market. The lack of success is probably due to the following constraints of the medium:

The relatively small amount of data that can be stored on a diskette compared to a CD.

The time required to load and search multiple diskettes.

The increased potential to "lose" a part of a set.

For readers old enough to remember, the analogy can be made between diskettes and the old 33-1/3 LPs and 45s. Imagine the inconvenience of listening to a broadway show using a dozen 45s rather than a single LP! The diskette medium causes the same level of inconvenience.

The "inconvenience" and potential loss of data are minimized if the data are distributed on a network. In such cases, the diskette medium has appeal if (1) it provides very current data and can be positioned successfully against online access to the retrospective data; or (2) it provides data critical to the library's clientele that cannot be as easily searched through another medium. The information provider must weigh the diskette benefits against the negative attributes of the medium and assess the net results in terms of the library's information and technology needs.

End User Market

The end user market has always existed among faculty, students, researchers, and consumers, who, for years, have been requesting the services of librarians/information specialists to find answers to their questions. Information providers have not historically marketed directly to the ultimate users of their data because it was difficult, if not impossible, to identify and reach them. The barriers between the two groups, however, have begun to crumble for the reasons stated earlier. Although the walls are not completely obliterated and, occasionally, the transitional debris makes it difficult to identify and contact the appropriate groups easily, the attempt to do so is well advised. A warning, however, must be posted.

It is tempting to become overly optimistic in viewing the sales potential of the end user market. It is estimated that, at the end of 1988, there were 66 million potential buyers of information in the U.S. workforce (professionals, managers, sales, technical staff, service workers).[33] At the same time, however, there were only 20 million installed PCs in U.S. businesses. If these PCs were not routinely shared, a large portion of U.S. workers could very well have remained illiterate in the computer and electronic products area.

When marketing information, the information provider must remember that librarian/-information specialists are easy to identify. These are the professionals who know about databases and their design, understand how to develop questions to maximize retrieval with minimal complications, and are well versed in the information tools available. Their search skills are fine tuned by the frequency of application--but not so the end users! Even if the end user target market can be clearly defined, e.g., organic chemists or psychologists, it is extremely difficult to determine the percentage of that market that is computer literate and actually able to use the product.

Online

Locating end users is not an easy task. The majority of information providers offer their databases online indirectly to customers through a host system or vendor. As a result, the providers are frequently barred from access to the names/addresses of the system users because they are viewed as proprietary customers of the vendor not the information provider.

An additional major stumbling block to online searching for inexperienced users is the software/search command language.[34] This language is often intimidating and discouraging for the users; a poor understanding of the search protocols can lead to equally poor search results, which do not encourage the prospect of a repeat experience.

Another factor inhibiting end user searching is the traditional online pricing structure. With the meter running, even experienced searchers strive to limit online search time. Despite these hurdles, the information provider can reach the end users via a three-pronged approach: (1) direct contact, (2) contact via the intermediary, and (3) contact via the vendor.

Direct Access

Exhibit at end user meetings/conventions. (Invite end users to visit the booth through an ad in the meeting program.)

Create an awareness of the database through judiciously placed space ads in relevant journals. (*A note of caution*: spend promotional dollars wisely-- ads create awareness but revenue generation is difficult to track.)

Hold workshops in conjunction with society meetings.

Provide strong customer support. (The users will call the database producer for help.)

Distribute an end user-oriented newsletter to contact names.

Issue press releases to announce new files and/or enhancements.

Present product reviews at online meetings.

Develop or contract to have developed a user friendly program with a search language that interfaces with the databases for ease of access.

Access Through Intermediary

Develop an onsite training/education program.

Provide the intermediary with education tools, e.g., slides, tapes, fact sheets, sample searches, quick guides, posters.

Access Through Vendor

Participate in vendor training sessions.

Publish articles/ads in vendor newsletters.

Develop direct mail campaigns. (The vendor will mail producer materials to its customer base.)

Establish non-peak hour pricing.

Create inexpensive training files to encourage practice.

Develop online end user features, interfaces, and displays.

It serves to remember that end users rarely become conversant with the multitude of search protocols available among vendors--users usually limit their access to only one or two vendors. If possible, information providers should distribute their data through all vendors appropriate to the given target market.

Another fact to be aware of is that the largest growth (211.5%) in online subscribers from 1984-88 was for general reference interest files on such services as CompuServe, GEnie, and Prodigy.[35] If an information provider has data that could be categorized as "general interest," the end user market may be worth pursuing for the long term.

CD-ROM

End user acceptance of CD-ROM products has occurred much earlier in the life cycle of that medium than with online. This acceptance is due to the increased computer literacy of the public and the savvy of the information providers--for the most part, the software interfaces for CDs have been user friendly from the outset.

The end users referred to are those in a library/information center/academic department setting. After some initial training, the users bypass the intermediary to perform their own searches on CD-ROM. While they eagerly use the products, the end users are not yet widely purchasing them. They cannot justify the hardware expenditures required, much less the database fees, for occasional searching. The CD-ROM installation scenario differs from online where, for the modest price of a modem, and possibly a user friendly software interface, end users who own a PC can access hundreds of databases whenever the need arises.

It is too early to predict accurately, but a safe assumption is that as new stand alone CDs (those without print counterparts) are introduced, prices will gradually become more affordable (indeed, this has been the trend since 1987).[36] In a few years, the more sophisticated end users will, more than likely, purchase select CDs related to their work much as they purchase related print references today.

Information providers should not necessarily defer marketing CDs to end users. Marketing can have several positive outcomes: (1) end users will put pressure on the librarian to purchase the product; (2) groups of end users (in an academic, research, or business environment) will pool budget resources to purchase the product; and (3) sophisticated end users will buy affordable CDs that contain highly relevant data.

Targeted subsets of data, such as those distributed by Cambridge Scientific Abstracts, have significant potential in the end user market. Information providers should begin developing packaged portions of data on CD-ROM for the end user market.

The same hurdles discussed for selling CD-ROM to the library market apply here as well: installed hardware base, networking (among groups of end users), legal issues, computer literacy, etc. The approaches to overcoming these hurdles also remain the same. How can the end users be reached? The following approaches have proven successful:

> Direct mail (including a response form) to the target audience. Careful mail list selection is critical; telemarketing follow up can help close the sale.

> Cold call telemarketing. Again, success is directly related to the selected lists.

> Space ads and press releases to create product awareness.

> Exhibits/workshops at relevant end user meetings.

Working with the intermediaries to reach their end users also expedites product acceptance.

Diskette

The diskette medium is well suited to end user audiences for the following reasons:

> Manageable quantities of data can be distributed, even weekly, on two or three diskettes.

> Replication costs do not inhibit weekly or biweekly updates.

> The product can be priced at rates perceived as affordable by end users, with data amounts and publication frequency reasonably balanced.

> Reasonably computer literate users are familiar with the diskette medium. (On the down side, computer illiterate customers will place a very heavy burden on the technical support staff.)

119

Diskette marketing issues remain identical for any electronic product: size of installed hardware base, need for license agreements, networking policies, etc. In addition, the issue of pirating is of prime concern. While the time involved in photocopying print products has inhibited widespread abuse and/or the use of a routing list may have motivated readers to purchase their own print copy, diskettes lend themselves to easy, cheap, and relatively quick duplication. Information providers may want to add this potential abuse factor into their pricing equation.

Forceful marketing of the diskette product to the end user can be achieved directly by the information provider via direct mail, telemarketing, and exhibits. Tactics are analogous to those employed for CD-ROM and online. Because end users represent a larger, potential market universe for a product as compared to librarians/information specialists, the response rates (and ultimate payment rates) will be lower than with the library market.
Also, due to the potentially large audience, trial programs, in which more than one diskette edition is shipped, could prove to be costly. Sample issues or demo diskettes are the most cost effective methods for providing end users with hands on experience prior to final sale.

What "sells" end users on a diskette product? Benefits to be promoted are primarily search speed, lack of telecommunications charges, and the ability to download data directly for personal use if the users have a file management package. Reduced search time improves overall work productivity.

Note: The ongoing support of end users' electronic products is not trivial (*see* the following section on Customer Service). An information provider directly entering the end user market must be well prepared for the consequences.

Multi-Party Purchase--Magnetic Tapes

The sales and marketing of data on magnetic tape are long and arduous processes due to the contractual agreements required and the number of (and diverse requirements of) the parties involved, e.g., end users, librarian/information specialists, data processing staff, purchasing agents, and lawyers--at the very least. Magnetic tapes have a targeted audience--individual libraries and information centers or consortia of such groups that possess the required software/hardware and the excess computer capacity (in run time) to operate an interactive search service and/or process batch searches.

Space ads, direct mail, etc., play no part here; the tape lease process is essentially a direct contact sales effort with frequent communication throughout. An organization's need for the data is usually the driving force for the sale; this need surfaces in one of two ways: (1) the demand is created by the end users or information intermediaries within the organization due to heavy online use of the data; or (2) the demand is created by the information provider, which "sells" its data to the end users/librarians through an onsite presentation that matches the potential customers' needs to the product features and benefits. Obviously, the former situation is the easier sale--the potential customers already use and want the data. The latter situation requires more time and should be supported by offering both a sample tape for use during a limited time period and at least one education seminar. Issues that must be considered are:

> **Users' Expectations:** Why do users want the data? How will the data be distributed, and who will have access to them?

> **Hardware/Software Requirements:** Do the customers have the internal capabilities to load the tapes and run them?

> **Authorization Levels:** Who has final sign-off approval on the sale and the license agreement?

> **Support:** How much support--both before and after the sale--is required?

> **Revenue Stream:** What is the payoff between the long term commitment on the part of the customers versus the up-front time investment from the information provider's staff?

> **Legal Issues:** How do the users' expectations and the information providers' copyright needs mesh or conflict (networking, site licensing, data usage)?

The tape license sales approach is consultative in nature--on every issue (data, usage, hardware, etc.)--and can take at least six months or more. Revenues from tape licenses, especially for large files, can be substantial. Due to the lengthy sales process revolving around multiple issues, the customer will have given serious thought to the long term ramifications of the purchase. The drawn out process usually infers that the sale represents a serious commitment, and renewal rates are normally high.

Customer Support

The area that is commonly neglected in discussions of the implications of electronic distribution if that of customer support. Because the majority of information providers already have established help desks and training programs supporting their online and print products, it is frequently assumed that the status quo is adequate. In reality, it is not.

Implications

The skills required to support CD-ROM and diskette products are quite different from those required for online and print support. In this section, the experiences of the Institute for Scientific Information(ISI) will be used as a case study to demonstrate the changes and shifts in customer support necessitated by requirements of an era of changing technology.

ISI is a major provider of secondary information products across all scientific disciplines as well as in the social sciences and humanities. It has been offering print products since 1960, and online/magnetic tape products since the early 70s. In 1988, ISI introduced the Science Citation Index(SCI) on CD-ROM, followed shortly thereafter in the same year by Current Contents on Diskette/Life Sciences Edition. Since then, ISI has launched the compact disk edition of the Social Sciences Citation Index(SSCI), diskette versions of five other editions of Current Contents and a biweekly diskette product entitled Focus On: Global Change.

In the last two years, ISI's revenues from print products have diminished from 82% of corporate totals to 62% estimated for 1990, while electronic revenues have grown from 11% in 1988 to an estimated 25% in 1990. The almost instantaneous market acceptance of the electronic products has been gratifying, but it has had a significant impact on the help desk, which had not been prepared for the onslaught of calls.

In the past, the help desk staff had to answer questions about print products (content, features, price) and online services (content, search techniques and differences among vendors). These types of products were also supported through educational lectures, fact sheets, slide sets, posters, sample searches, and reprints of usage related papers written by customers, themselves.

With the release of CD-ROM and diskette products, the face of customer support changed quickly. The most dramatic change was in the level of phone activity, which increased 72% from 1987 to 1988, and 105% from 1988 to 1989. From January through August 1990, the activity increased 191% over that in the same time period in 1989. (*see* Figure 8)

The level of activity was not the only change. (*see* Figure 9) In fact, that increase, in and of itself, would not have resulted in significant problems. It was the increased activity combined with a major shift in the type of questions and the customer profile that posed difficulties.

Calls to the help desk were no longer content and features oriented. They resulted from the customer experiencing a problem with or simply not understanding how to use the product. This was a new experience for the help desk staff. No one had ever called to find out how to turn a page or read a book. Now the help desk was inundated with questions on how to solve technical problems.

Help Desk Activity

Quarter	1988	1989	1990	%
1	522	761	2,086	300%
2	434	608	1,822	320%
3	686	1,257	2,811	310%
4	718	2,099	2,400(est)	234%
Total:	2,360	4,725	9,119(est)	286%*

*A 581% increase since 1987 - before CD/diskettes were introduced.

-figure 8 -

<u>MAJOR CHANGES</u>

- Number of Questions

- Types of Questions

- Level of Detail Required

- Diversity of Callers

- Length of Phone Call per Inquiry

-figure 9-

Many of the calls required in-depth analysis (up to twenty questions' worth) of hardware configuration and software questions. The standard length of phone call per inquiry increased from five to nine minutes. For every two inbound phone calls, one return call was required, lasting an average of twenty minutes.

The diversity of callers also broadened. In the past, most inquiries were from information specialists and librarians. Calls began coming in from doctors' secretaries, bench scientists--in short, the entire spectrum from hackers to the computer illiterate. Each electronic product elicited its own set of medium specific questions, although queries for CD-ROM and diskette were quite similar.

Magnetic Tape

The customer support issues for tapes fall into four categories: (1) documentation, (2) software/hardware recommendations, (3) file design, and (4) use policies. When customers acquire data on magnetic tape for in-house use, they are demonstrating a high level of interest in the raw data. They may want to manipulate and massage the information according to their own specifications. The provision of clear, concise documentation on every record and searchable field is absolutely essential, even more so as the customers move from batch SDI services to an interactive searching environment.

Tape customers will request recommendations on software and hardware if they are building a totally new system. On this topic, the ISI support group is neutral, merely supplying information on what is available and whom to contact.

File design and policy details are closely related. Tape customers tend to use more of the available fields than do the online vendors. As a result, they scrutinize the data closely. Bibliographic rules, abbreviations, categorizations--all are routinely questioned, and the provider's rationale for the methodology must be consistent, clear, and practical.

Perhaps the most troublesome area for customer support is the varying degree of customer expectations with regards to quality, content, and specific application of the data. Practical support and advice on these aspects are the glue for a satisfactory long term relationship between the provider and the customer.

As mentioned earlier, with tapes distributed through an outside program such as BRS OnSite, the burden on customer support declines but does not disappear. Only the information providers are intimately familiar with their data and can satisfactorily answer detailed questions, particularly those about indexing policy.

CD-ROM/Diskette

The customer support issues for CD-ROM and diskette are very similar and fall into three categories: (1) equipment related, (2) networks, and (3) site licenses, with the former predominating by far. Questions on equipment vary from the very simple--e.g., What CD-ROM drives are compatible with the product? What is the storage capacity required?--to the more complex, e.g., How do I get my printer to work? With the hundreds of possible hardware configurations that exist, the support staff literally have to walk customers through the process. This requirement can take quite a long time and is particularly laborious when the customers' phone is far from the workstation.

Some of the most frequent hardware problems will result from the fact that MS-DOS extensions do not support the complexities of a multi-disk drive environment. Support staff must be thoroughly versed in this potential pitfall and know exactly what can and cannot be remedied. End user products, such as those distributed on diskette, appear to generate the most inquiries to the help desk; this pattern is increasing. (*see* Figure 10)

Diskette products introduce distinct problems. The complications inherent to supporting a diskette arise from the number of format variations that can exist--Mac, IBM, NEC, 5.25" low density, 5.25" high density, and 3.5" low density. The number of diskettes shipped to customers varies with the amount of data published during that period and the density of the diskette requested. Even this kind of variation confuses the novice end user and will generate a phone call.

Shift in Support Requirements

The customer support required for electronic products, particularly for the end user electronic products, is quite different from that required for print products. The major issues to be addressed are outlined in Figure 11. At ISI, the volume and length of the phone calls have necessitated an increase in staff. The impact of a labor increase can, however, be minimized by reallocating the activities of the support staff, e.g., decreasing the number of individual online lectures and increasing help desk support hours. Customer support staff flexibility is critical.

800 Lines

With the increased number of inquiries, the number of phone lines at ISI had to increase. A new system was installed, and the help desk is now supported by a total of four phones. An 800 number directs the customers to ISI where a "menu" leads them to the help desk. The desk is manned by two to four people, depending upon the volume of calls. Before 9:00 am and after 5:00 pm (Philadelphia, PA time), customers can leave messages on an answering machine. European calls are handled by the ISI UK office in Uxbridge.

While the number of calls has been fairly consistent over time, staff must be prepared for periods when new products or upgrades are released. The number of phone calls at such times can increase by as much as 170%. The number of phone lines as well as the

Product Analysis

	__1989__	__1990__
Print:	6%	4%
Online:	31%	21%
CDROM:	10%	7%
Diskette:	52%	64%
Other:	1%	4%

-figure 10-

SHIFTS IN REQUIREMENTS

- **Staffing**
  - Number
  - Qualifications

- **Training**

- **Agent Support**

- **800 Numbers**

- **Documentation**
  - Level of Detail
  - Ease of Use

- **Customer Inquiry System**

- **Reports/Forms**

-figure 11 -

hours of "live" phone coverage must also be continually evaluated to ensure that customers are able to get through.

Training

Customer training for CD-ROM and diskette products varies in complexity. Similar to online and print products, content and features remain an integral focus of training. The major training effort with regard to CD-ROM and diskette, however, is directed to equipment issues. Typical questions are: What hardware configuration is required? How is the software installed? How are the data loaded? How are results printed?

In the past, customers knew how to open the book and find the index. Diskette/-CD-ROM customers, however, must be taught how to "open" the product and find various sections of the electronic "book." Each medium has its own specific problem area, e.g., 21% of the diskette questions are load related as compared to 6% of the CD-ROM questions, while 53% of the CD questions are related to installation as compared to 10% of the diskette questions. Search related questions are about the same percent (8%) for each product type. With online, 53% of the questions are search related.

Onsite training for diskettes (which are usually low priced) is not cost effective; most issues can be resolved with a well written manual. Onsite training for CD-ROM is not absolutely essential. CD-ROM purchases usually represent a significant investment for a library, and onsite training can promote usage, thereby improving the chances for renewal. Ultimately, information providers must exercise judgment as to when a site visit for training is recommended. (Staff/travel expenses must be weighed against the potential revenue stream).

As a natural extension of training, the agents who represent publishers and market their electronic products must be computer literate. This is not a requirement for book and journal agents (or sellers). The hazard is that agents can be technologically "out of date." This situation can then pose an additional problem, since the customers, particularly those in locations geographically distant from the publisher, rely on the agent for technical assistance.

Documentation

Documentation is a necessary evil for an electronic product. A user manual is an essential element of the product package, although the probability of a user ever reading it is extremely low. The manual, if used, is actually the first line of defense in handling problems once a product has been released. The manual must be easy to read, logically arranged, and contain every possible level of detail--from the most basic use to the most sophisticated and complex--with lots of "visual aids."

The index to the manual is another important element. It must include terminology that will lead both the naive users and the most competent hackers to the information they require. User manuals should also be equipped with separate quick guides (e.g., laminated cards that contain the most utilized prompts) for daily use at the users' workstation.

Even the best written user documentation may remain in its virgin state, virtually untouched, into perpetuity. The product must, therefore, contain built-in help screens; the support staff must acquire a sense of humor ... but more about the humor later.

Query Support Systems

Due to the diversity of questions and the number of calls, a PC-based customer inquiry system is an important component of ongoing customer support. The call record in Figure 12 lists what kinds of data should be captured. The PC system captures data and allows ongoing analysis of the questions being asked (type, frequency, etc.). Such an analysis is essential for an accurate identification of customer needs; future upgrades can then include the improvements/features that customers actually want.

The query system also provides fodder for newsletter material and for lists of frequently asked questions (and answers) that can be distributed to customers. To expedite call activities, guidelines can be included in the user manual to prepare customers to gather the required information in advance of their phone calls. (*see* Figure 13)

Staff Requirements

The support of electronic products requires a new level of skills and knowledge from the help desk staff at ISI. These requirements include:

Detailed product knowledge about print, online, CD/diskette, tape, and all other services.

Computer literacy about hardware/software, set-up, etc.

Understanding of corporate policies underlying licensing, networking, downloading, and pricing.

Strong interpersonal Skills.

Patience.

Sense of humor.

Implications

TECHNICAL HELP DESK CALL RECORD

DATE: 90/_____ /_____ **At** _____ :_____ (use 24 hr. clock)   **STAFF:** _____

ANSWERED: SAME OR 90/ _____ / _____ **Resolution time:**_____ minutes

CUSTOMER _____

Co/Inst _____

Address _____

City _____ State _____ Zip _____

Phone (_____) _____ Country _____

CIS #_____ FAX _____

QUERY _____

_____

_____

_____

REPLY _____

_____

_____

Please fill this in correctly, use the right codes:

PRODUCT   *Online*_____ *CD-ROM*_____ *Software*_____

Print _____ *Other Products* _____

QUERY TYPE   *Search*_____ *CR*_____ *Install*_____ *Load*_____ *Export*_____ *P-RAP*_____

*Print*_____ *Enhance*_____ *Document*_____ *Sale/Price*_____ *Info/Cover*_____ *Other*_____

Summary_____

_____

FOLLOW-UP

REFERRED TO: Telmark_____ CustSvs_____ Other _____

COPY TO: _____

FULFILLMENT: Y☐ N☐   **NEWSLETT?** Y☐ N☐   **BUG/ENHANCE FORM?** Y☐ N☐

SEND: SJL for _____ Online Kit   CRQG

Other _____

PREF RATE? Y☐ N☐   Form sent to: Customer ____ / ____ / 90   BSC ____ / ____ / 90

Follow Up Done 90/____/____   By _____   Revised [8/16/90]

-figure 12-

131

Customer Guidelines

When you call, please be prepared to supply the following information to the Help Desk representative:

- Description of problem, including any error messages

- Your name, telephone number, and when you can be reached

- PC brand and model

- CD-ROM drive brand and model

- Number of CD-ROM drives attached to this PC

- Version of DOS

- Version of MS-DOS CD-ROM Extensions

- Contents of CONFIG.SYS and AUTOEXEC.BAT files.

  (To print the contents of these files, from the root directory of your hard drive, type **TYPE CONFIG.SYS >PRN** and press Return, then type **TYPE AUTOEXEC.BAT >PRN** and press Return.)

Calling from a phone at or near the workstation where you are having the problem will simplify the troubleshooting process greatly!

Copyright © 1990 Institutefor Scientific Information ®(ISI ®) reproduced with permission of ISI.

-figure 13 -

132

Product knowledge is a given for help desk staff. They must be familiar with each of the product's features, benefits, and usage. The introduction of electronic products has imposed another layer of essential knowledge upon the staff--computer literacy. Such computer literacy implies that staff have to understand how computers communicate and know what to do when that communication fails. They have to ask the right investigative questions, then walk the novice users through the entire problem solving process.

A minimum of three months staff product training is required (assuming that the computer basics are already in place). The new hire should view and absorb product knowledge from product presentations given at various levels internally before going "live" at the help desk or at users' sites. During the three or four months following training, new staff must still be monitored to ensure that they are providing correct answers and actually helping the customers.

The help desk staff should actively and frequently interface with the product development group, not only to provide customer feedback but also to become familiar with the new products being developed. The support staff should be knowledgeable about every dimension of a product before it is released; they can also serve as an expert, readily accessible, in house Beta test market for new products. As the customer spokesperson, they would more naturally know the features and improvements that would satisfy the customers.

Support staff are responsible for other areas of expertise. They more than just solve problems, although that is a major component of their job. They are also expected to be well versed in such areas as pricing, policy (licensing, networking, and downloading), and general company information. Patience is more than a virtue in this job; it is an absolute job requirement, along with good people skills and a strong, untiring, unlimited sense of humor. The staff are no longer talking chiefly to information professionals. Many end user callers are computer illiterate and have no notion of what to do with a diskette or CD-ROM.

Currently, six people support the ISI help desk activities and training for approximately 75 products and services, more than half of which are in electronic format. The staff include one lecturer, one documentation writer, three technical help desk staff, and a manager. All perform some level of help desk support, particularly during the busy periods. On a regular basis, a core of three handles the help desk activities (65% of their time spent on the phone, 25% on report writing, and 10% on sanity retention). The manager, lecturer, and documentation specialist contribute time to the help desk as demand requires.

133

Ongoing Trends

Customer support operations will feel the impact of ongoing trends in the information industry. These trends are an increased number of end users who are neither computer nor information literate; changes in technology that must be monitored so that hardware/software questions can be intelligently answered; a continued increase in the volume of inquiries; and the need for more easy to use support tools.

It is certainly not cost effective to continue to add support staff linearly as the volume of sales increases. While, indirectly, the customer support staff are linked to revenue (they help keep the customer satisfied and raise the chance of renewal), the link is difficult to quantify during budget reviews. It is more economical to improve the product, itself, thereby reducing the need for customer support altogether. The product design is particularly critical to the ease of use of the end users. The product should be simple to use and have a generous amount of help screens. A fine balance must be maintained between the simplicity of design desired by the unsophisticated end users and the power and speed features desired by the more experienced searchers.

Another line of defense easing the burden on customer support is user support tools such as well written manuals, simple quick guides, and even newsletters that can provide helpful hints and updates on usage and problem solving tactics. The final line of defense is the technical help desk. Unfortunately, many customers will start there first.

This aspect of customer behavior cannot be overlooked, particularly when electronic products are involved. If the customers cannot access the information that they want, even if the obstacle is equipment failure or lack of technical expertise, the information provider faces disgruntled customers and a possible erosion in renewals.

If a producer is moving from print to electronic media, the customer support team must be involved in that shift before the electronic products are released. A recent article[37] discussed user expectations in regard to customer support. Granted, the article was discussing support of software packages, not information products, but the customers will doubtlessly act the same in both cases. The article stated that customers expect the following:

> Free, unlimited technical support.

> Telephone access to the vendor. (Electronic bulletin boards are nice, but a live human being is better!)

> Intelligent help desk staff.

In the final analysis, customers expect service--clear and simple. If they do not get it from one information provider, they will take their business elsewhere. According to James H. Sweetland, " ... the survivors in this industry will not be those with the fanciest gadgets or the most colors on the screen but those who actually pay attention to the customers after the sale."[38]

Legal Issues

In the days of print information, the major concern of publishers was copyright protection to prevent pirating (via photocopying, etc.). Publishers were not concerned about how many end users in an organization accessed the printed information. There was certainly little concern thirty years ago about users taking all of the information from Chemical Abstracts or a Science Citation Index, manipulating it and creating a derivative work. The advent of photocopiers did raise concerns, particularly among primary publishers, hence the development of the Copyright Clearance Center (CCC) to promote photocopying within the framework of the copyright law and provide financial remuneration to the copyright owner.

The advent of electronic publishing, however, did raise a new set of concerns: downloading (retrieval and local storage of data from machine readable databases), networking of diskettes and CD-ROMs, dial access to networked products, etc. In an era of mergers and acquisitions, it is conceivable that multiple sales of CDs or magnetic tapes to a variety of organizations could ultimately dwindle to a single sale with dial access. This forecast may be extreme, but it conveys some idea of the information provider's concerns.

While each new medium opens up new markets, it also cannibalizes the subscriber base from the other existing media. The information provider must exercise sound judgment in predicting what portion of the current, aggregate subscriber base will migrate to the new medium. With that portion of the subscribers in mind, ownership and usage of the information contained on electronic media are commonly protected by license agreements that outline the rights and obligations of both licensor and licensee.

This section alerts the reader to the issues that should be tracked; it is not, however, comprehensive in its coverage of legal issues. For further reference, the reader should consult two excellent NFAIS works on this subject.[39,40] (*see* Figure 14)

Copyright

Copyright is the exclusive legal right to reproduce and sell the matter and form of a literary, musical, or artistic work. Copyright is secured when "...original works of authorship are fixed in any tangible medium of expression, now known or later developed,

Legal Issues

- **What is Copyright ?**

  - Who owns it ?
  - For how Long ?
  - Is it transferable ?
  - What is " Fair Use " ?
  - Can a Database be protected ?

- **What is Downloading ?**

  - How can it be monitored ?
  - What steps can be taken to control it ?

- **What is Networking ?**

  - Who can access it ?
  - How many simultaneous users does it accomodate ?
  - Is off-site access available ?

- **What is a Gateway ?**

  - How is copyright/ownership protected ?
  - What are gateway-specific issues ?

- **What is a License Agreement ?**

  - What should it include ?
  - Is there an " ideal " agreement ?

Bottom Line : How are the mutual rights and obligations of the information provider, user, and vendor(where appropriate) satisfactorily covered?

-figure 14-

from which they can be perceived, reproduced, or otherwise communicated, either directly or with the aid of a machine or device." (U.S. Copyright Act, Section 102 of Chapter 1 of Title 17) The original owner of the copyright is the creator of the work unless the work is a "work made for hire"--a commissioned work or one created by an employee within the scope of his/her employment. Copyright lasts for the life of the creator plus 50 years. For a "work made for hire," the term of duration is 75 years from creation or 100 years from publication, whichever is shorter. Copyright can be transferred through written notice on the part of the owner.

Although copyright registration and/or notice is not required for members of the Berne Convention[41] (the United States joined Berne in 1989), both are strongly advised. (Notice must be used for all U.S. works created before the United States joined the Convention.) Standard notice is as follows: the copyright symbol (a "C" in a circle), the year of publication, and the name of the copyright owner, e.g., "Copyright © 1991 National Federation of Abstracting and Information Services."

The reader should adhere to the following guidelines:

Protect all products--print and electronic--via copyright notice.

When in doubt about copyright ownership and usage (e.g., inclusion in a database of author abstracts from primary journals), obtain legal counsel. The definition of "fair use" (Sections 107 and 108 of the U.S. Copyright Act) is vague!

Deposit two copies of all information products with the Library of Congress within three months of publication. Although copyright registration and notice are optional, deposits to the Library of Congress are required. Copies can be demanded by the Library of Congress and failure to comply can result in a fine.[42] This rule applies to both printed and electronic products.

Define the term, "database" (in answer to the questions: Is a database a "compilation"? Does it constitute an "original" work of authorship?). Registration of a database for copyright protection can be complex.[43-45] Obtain legal advice to ensure that an information product is qualified for and receives proper protection.

The complexities of copyright law are substantial. If the reader wishes to become familiar with the basic issues, recommended reading is the text, *Modern Copyright Fundamentals*, by Ben Weil and Barbara Polansky, American Society for Information Science, 1989, published by Learned Information, Inc.

Downloading

Downloading is most commonly defined as taking data in machine readable form from a database that is available either online or through other electronic media and storing them in a local device for future manipulation and use. Downloading can also refer to the capture of printed material via scanning or rekeying.

The information provider should develop a downloading policy that limits usage (by whom, how, at what price, how distributed--internally by information brokers, customers, etc.), reporting requirements and fees. If the data are being distributed via a vendor (e.g., online files), the provider's downloading policy must be included in the license agreement, and proper notification given to the ultimate users of the system.[40]

Networking

A local area network (LAN) is a system of computers linked together to share software, data and equipment. Through such a system, data diskettes and CD-ROMs can be simultaneously accessed by multiple users. These systems have become fairly widespread in academia and industry, alike, and information specialists/librarians in these environments prefer to license an electronic product that can be networked.

Since network capabilities can affect multiple sales of a given product, networked information is usually priced higher than the standard product. Network usage is governed by a separate network agreement. The information provider must develop a policy that will cover who can use the network, how many simultaneous users can access it (price gradations can be offered for 1-10 users, 10-25 users, etc.), whether or not dial access is permitted, etc.[40]

Gateway

A gateway is broadly defined as a link(s) between a user of an online database and the primary host system(s) of the database.[46] One example of a gateway is a front end system, with the front end being either a software package or a system such as Telebase's EasyNet. While a gateway can certainly heighten the awareness and usage of a database, it introduces problems as well, e.g., an unlicensed host may access a database for which it has no contractual agreement or users may not be aware of the database ownership, or usage restrictions, or which host system they are accessing.

The NFAIS Code of Practice for Gateways outlines the rights and obligations of each member of the gateway information chain--information providers, host systems, gateway operators, and end users--in regard to ownership, quality, usage, user identification, etc.

(A copy can be obtained from NFAIS Headquarters). If the information provider wants to build in restrictions to gateway access to a database, such restrictions must be included in the license agreement with the host system(s) vending the file.[40]

License Agreement

A license agreement documents, in writing, the elements of a business deal. It outlines obligations, rights, prices, delivery terms--the traditional elements of any business transaction. The unique feature of this type of transaction, however, is that there is no transfer of ownership. The information provider retains copyright (ownership) of the data being licensed. All of the aforementioned areas--downloading, networking, and gateways--should be clarified by the license.

Drafting a legal document that meets the needs of everyone in the information chain is, indeed, a challenge. Items that should be included in the license are:

Statement of the parties involved in the agreement (licensor/licensee).

Scope of the agreement/in general terms.

Definition of the terms used in the agreement.

Explanation of proprietary rights and copyright notice.

License grant (exclusive/nonexclusive).

Payment terms (license fee, royalties, hit charges, downloading fees, etc.).

Payment frequency.

Usage reports.

Audits.

Timing of data delivery.

Marketing/training (e.g., free time on vendor system).

Warranties (liabilities, indemnifications).

Assignment of the license.

Excused defaults.

Term of the agreement.

Arbitration in the event of disagreement.

Waiver of contractual obligations.

Confidentiality.

Severability.

Governing Law.

Integration and incorporation.

Each of the preceding elements is not relevant to every transaction, e.g., marketing and training are not necessarily appropriate for a CD-ROM license to a library. All elements should, however, be considered during the drafting of any license agreement. The reader should refer to references 39 and 40 for further details and samples of representative agreements.

Flexibility is key. While both the information provider and the user of the data may envision the "ideal" license agreements, it is guaranteed that these ideals will differ. Copyright protection is important (legal counsel is essential here); flexibility is equally critical. An agreement is never ideal if it prohibits sales.

Summary

Electronic publishing carries major risks and opportunities for the information provider. The long term rewards of selling electronic information, particularly in the end user market, can be quite satisfying if the challenges are met within the framework of a solid business strategy that is supported by both a sound pricing scheme and complementary license agreements. The issues raised in this chapter must be viewed in the larger context of overall business objectives. The ten commandments of electronic publishing (*see* Figure 15) lead the way.

Ten Commandments of Electronic Publishing

End-user markets are demanding and time-consuming - don't open the door unless you are prepared!

Learning curves for the use of electronic products are indirectly proportional to the need for the information provided - *the greater the need, the shorter the curve.*

Electronic products *must* bear their fair share of database creation costs.

Contractual agreements *must* balance the protection of mutual rights while minimizing customer intimidation

Technological advances must be *diligently monitored* - for product development as well as for customer support

Retrieval software must be *perceived* as simple, straightforward and easy to use - keep complexities transparent to the user

Optimal packaging of information medium and price varies by customer need - know the target market *before* venturing in

Never underestimate the computer *illiteracy* of the end-user

Information pricing must be *technology-independent* - the medium is simply a source of more-or-less "value added".

Customer support *is critical* to a product's success and its importance cannot be over-emphasized

-figure 15-

References

1. Seals, Jr., J.V. 1990. "The Past as Prologue." ACS paper presented at Infobase '90.

2. *Electronic Information Industry Forecast North America 1989-1994.* 1990. New York: Link Resources Corporation, July 1990, in press.

3. Goldstein, M. 1989. "Pricing Strategies." *Information Marketing Handbook.* Philadelphia: NFAIS. 59.

4. Hawkins, D.T. 1987. "The Commodity Nature of Information." *ONLINE.* January, 1987: 67.

5. *The U.S. Market for Online Databases.* 1988. New York: Frost and Sullivan: 2.

6. Garman, N. 1990. "Dialog Discusses Pricing: An Interview with Dialog's President Roger K. Summit." *ONLINE.* January 1990: 40.

7. Tenopir. C. 1988. "Is Connect-Time Pricing Obsolete?" *Library Journal.* March 1, 1988: 48.

8. Harry, J. and D. Kaser. 1989. "The Real Online Pricing Dilemma." *CAS Report.* No. 27, Fall 1989.

9. *ibid*: 2.

10. Seals, Jr., J.V. 1990. "The Past as Prologue." *Infobase '90 Proceedings.*

11. Hawkins, D.T. 1989. "In Search of Ideal Information Pricing." *ONLINE.* March 1989: 19.

12. Jack, R.F. 1990. "The New ESA/IRS Pricing Scheme: A Comparison with Dialog." *ONLINE.* January 1990: 35.

13. Garman, N. 1990. "Online Pricing: An Interview with Marino F. Saksida of ESA/IRS." *ONLINE.* January 1990: 30.

14. Johnson, M. and P. Walters. 1990. "Pricing for Information: The User's Point of View." *ONLINE.* January 1990: 31.

15. O'Leary, M. 1988. "Easynet Revisited: Pushing the Online Frontier." *ONLINE*. September 1988: 22.

16. Garman, N. 1990. "Dialog Discusses Pricing: An Interview with Dialog's President Roger K. Summit." *ONLINE*. January 1990: 40.

17. Garman, N. 1988. "Online Pricing: A Complex Maze not for Timid Mice." *Database*. April 1988: 6.

18. *Electronic Information Industry Forecast North America 1989-1994*. 1990. New York: Link Resources Corporation, July 1990, in press.

19. Helgerson, L., ed. 1989. *CD Data Report*. 6(2): 3.

20. *Information Industry Factbook*. 1989/90 edition. Stamford: Digital Information Group.

21. *Information Industry Bulletin*. 1990. Vol. 6(31). August 2, 1990: 1.

22. Rietdyk, R. 1990. "When is the Price Right? CD-ROM enters new Territory." *NFAIS Newsletter*. Vol. 32(11), November 1990: 133.

23. *Electronic Information Industry Forecast North America 1989-1994*. New York: Link Resources Corporation, July 1990, in press.

24. *Directory of Portable Databases*. New York: Cuadra/Elsevier. Vol. 1(1), January 1990.

25. *Directory of Portable Databases*. New York: Cuadra/Elsevier. Vol. 2(1), June 1990.

26. *Electronic Information Industry Forecast North America 1989-1994*. Link Resources Corporation, July 1990, in press.

27. Trudell, L. 1987. "Expanding End-User Access: Meeting the Marketing Challenge." *National Online Proceedings*. May 1987: 451.

28. Arnold, S.E. 1987. "End-Users: Dreams or Dollars." *ONLINE*. January 1987: 71.

29. *The Faxon Planning Report 1990*. 1989. The Faxon Press.

30. Havener, W.M. 1990. "Answering Ready Reference Questions: Print Versus Online." *ONLINE*. January 1990: 22.

31. Collines, A.M.K. 1989. "Financing CD-ROM: The Experience of a University Medical Library." *Program*. Vol. 23(4), 1989: 443.

32. *Information Industry Bulletin*. 1990. Vol. 6(20), May 17, 1990: 2.

33. *Information Industry Factbook*. 1989/1990 edition. Stamford: Digital Information Group: 230.

34. Basch, R. 1990. "Databank Software for the 1990's and Beyond - Part 1: The Users' Wish List." *ONLINE*. March 1990: 17.

35. *Information Industry Factbook*. 1989/1990 edition. Stamford: Digital Information Group: 230.

36. *ibid*: 301.

37. Furger, R. 1990. "Who Pays for Tech Support." *PC WORLD*. October 1990: 209.

38. Sweetland, J.H. 1990. "The Customer After the Sale." *Database*. April 1990: 6.

39. Bremner, J. and P. Miller. 1987. *Guide to Database Distribution: Legal Aspects and Model Contracts*. Philadelphia: NFAIS.

40. Schipper W. and B. Unruh, ed. 1989. *Information Industry Terms & Conditions*. Philadelphia: NFAIS.

41. Baumgarten, J.A. and C.A. Meyer. 1989. "Effects of U.S. Adherence to the Berne Convention." *IPA/STM Publishing Series*. No. 2.

42. Kozak, E.M. 1989. "New Copyright Law." *PUBLISH!* August 1989: 37.

43. Eisenshitz, T.S. 1989. "Copyright Laws and Online." *Journal of Information Science*. 15: 49.

44. Leonard, P.G. and P.A. Spender. 1989. "Copyright and Intellectual Property Protection of Databases." *Information Services & Use*. 9: 33.

45. Gardner, Carton & Douglas. 1990. "It's 3:00 A.M. Do you know where your Database Is?" *CLIPNOTES*. Vol. 4(2), August 1990.

46. NFAIS. 1987. *Gateway Code of Practices*. Philadelphia: NFAIS: 3.

Appendix

Appendix

Resource List

The resource list serves as a starting point for further research. A representative subset of vendors are listed--representing the types of products or services available.

For hardware and software, a review article is an excellent research source; all the major PC magazines include such articles. *PC World* and *PC Week* review articles are particularly helpful because they include "fact boxes" with vendor names, addresses, and phone numbers. Hardware and software are frequently distributed by dealers who may handle more than one vendor offering. Both dealers and service bureaus can be a good source of information. Some service bureaus are listed; for dealers the local yellow pages should be consulted under the listing, "computers."

CD/ROM

Pre-mastering and Mastering Facilities

American Helix Technology Corporation
1857 Colonial Village Lane
Lancaster, PA 17601
(717) 392-7840
(800) 525-6565

Digital Audio Disc Corporation (DADC)
1800 N. Fruitridge Avenue
Terre Haute, IN 47804
(812) 466-6821

DISC Manufacturing, Inc.
1120 Cosby Way
Anaheim, CA 92806
(714) 630-6700

Discovery Systems
7001 Discovery Blvd
Dublin, OH 43017
(614) 761-20000

Disctronics Inc.
3500 W. Olive Street
Suite 1020
Burbank, CA 91505
(714) 630-6700

Nimbus Information Systems, Inc.
P.O. Box 7305
Charlottesville, VA 22906
(800) 783-0778
(804) 985-1100

Philips/Dupont Optical Company 1409
Foulk Road
Suite 200
P.O. Box 7469
Wilmington, DE 19803-0469
(800) 433-DISC

SONY Recorded Media
655 River Oaks Parkway
San Jose, CA 95134
(408) 944-4220
or
One Indian Head Plaza
Nashua, NH 03060
(603) 595-4331
or
1800 North Fruitridge
Terre Haute, IN 47804
(812) 462-8160

3M Company
3M Optical Recording Department
3M Center St. Paul, MN 55144
(612) 733-5211

Professional Association

Optical Publishing Association
P.O. Box 21268
Columbus, OH 43221
(614) 793-9660

Resellers

Bureau of Electronic Publishing, Inc.
Dept L
141 New Road
Parsippany, NJ 07054
(800) 828-4ROM
(201) 808-2700

CD-ROM Inc
1667 Cole Blvd
Suite 400
Golden, CO 80401
(303) 231-9373
(consulting services available)

EBSCO Subscription Service
EBSCO Industries, Inc.
International Headquarters
P.O. Box 1943
Birmingham, AL 35201
(205) 991-6600

Peter J. Phethean, Ltd
1640 East Brookdale Avenue
La Habra, CA 90631
(213) 694-2112

Service Bureaus

American Helix Technology
Corporation
1857 Colonial Village Lane
Lancaster, PA 17601
(800) 525-6575

InfoService
Information Indexing, Inc.
12872 Valley View St. #11
Garden Grove, CA 92645
(714) 893-2471
(800) 888-0608

Knowledge Access, International
2685 Marine Way, Suite 1305
Mountain View, CA 94043
(800) 252-9273
(415) 969-0606

LaserData, Inc.
10 Technology Drive
Lowell, MA 01851
(617) 937-5900

Meridian Data, Inc.
5615 Scotts Valley Dr
Suite 200
Scotts Valley, CA 95066
(800) 755-8324
(408) 438-3100

NIMBUS Information Systems
P.O. Box 7305
Charlottesville, VA 22906
(804) 985-1100
(301) 948-2813

Online Products Corporation
Online Computer Systems, Inc.
20251 Century Boulevard
Germantown, MD 20874
(800) 922-9204
(301) 428-3700

Quantum Access, Inc.
50 Briar Hollow W., Suite 515
Houston, TX 77027
(713) 622-3211

Reference Technology, Inc.
5700 Flatiron Parkway
Boulder, CO 80301
(303) 449-4157
(800) 562-2015

TMS, Inc.
110 West Third Street
Stillwater, OK 74074
(405) 377-0880

Tri-Star Publishing
475 Virginia Drive
Fort Washington, PA 19034
(215) 641-6000

UniDisc
3941 Cherryvale Ave
Suite 1
Soquel, CA 95073
(408) 464-0707

Vendors

Compact Cambridge
7200 Wisconsin Avenue
Besthesda, MD 20814
(800) 843-7752

Dialog Information Services, Inc.
A Knight-Ridder Company
3460 Hillview Avenue
Palo Alto, CA 94304
(800) 334-2564

OCLC Online Computer Library
  Center, Inc.
6565 Franz Road
Dublin, OH 43017-0702
(614) 764-6000

SilverPlatter Information Inc. One
Newton Executive Park
Newton Lower Falls, MA 02162
(800) 343-0064

WilsonDisc
The H.W. Wilson Company
950 University Avenue
Bronx, NY 10452
(800) 367-6770
(212) 588-8400

DATA CONVERSION

Data Conversion Services

Access Innovations, Inc.
P.O. Box 40130
Albuquerque, NM 87196
(505) 265-3591

ASEC International, Inc.
11500 West Olympic Boulevard
Suite 400
Los Angeles, CA 90064
(213) 478-7755

Computership
International Data Services
One Wall Street Court
Suite 1001
New York, NY 10005
(800) 729-9714
(212) 509-9714

Input Center
Data Entry Service
320 N. Michigan
Suite 404
Chicago IL 60601
(312) 269-0272
(800) 624-8072

Saztec International, Inc
661 Moore Road
King of Prusia, PA 19406
(215) 337-8804

Quadrant Technologies, Inc.
Offshort Key Entry
P.O. Box 7788
Nashua, NH 03060
(603) 888-5969

Telemare Data Systems
25 North Broadway
Tarrytown, NY 10591
(914) 591-6255

Scanner Manufacturers

Calera Recognition Systems, Inc.
2500 Augustine Drive
Santa Clara, CA 95054
(408) 986-8006

Cannon USA Inc.
One Canon Plaza
Lake Success, NY 11042
(516) 488-6700

DEST Corporation
1015 E. Brokaw
San Jose, CA 95131
(408) 436-2700

IBM Corporation
Old Orchard Road
Armonk, NY 10504
(800) 447-4700

Kurzweil Computer Products
185 Albany Street
Cambridge, MA 02139
(617) 864-4700

Microteck Lab, Inc.
680 Knox Street
Torrance, CA 90502
(213) 321-2121

LOCAL AREA NETWORKS

CD-ROM Installation software

CD Diagnostics
American Helix Technology
Corporation
1857 Colonial Village Lane
Lancaster, PA 17601
(717) 392-7840
(800) 525-6575

CD-ROM Netware

CD Connection, CBIS CD Server
CBIS, Inc.
5875 Peachtree Ind. Blvd
Bldg 100, Unit 170
Norcross, GA 30092
(404) 446-1332

CD NET and DATAMAX
Meridian Data Inc
5616 Scotts Valley Drive
Scotts Valley, CA 95066
(408) 438-3100

LaserStar
Perceptics Corp
Westinghouse Electric Co
725 Pellissippi Pkwy
Box 22991
Knoxville, TN 37933-0991
(615) 966-9200

MAP Assist
Fresh Technology Group
1478 N. Tech Blvd 101
Gilbert, AZ 85234
(602) 497-4200

MultiPlatter
Silver Platter Information, Inc.
One Newton Executive Park
Newton Lower Falls, MA 02162-1449
(617) 969-2332
(800) 343-0064

Opti-Net
Online Computer Systems, Inc.
20251 Germantown Blvd
Germantown, MD 20874

CD-ROM PreMastering and Mastering Systems

CD Professional
Meridian Data Inc.
5616 Scotts Valley Drive
Scotts Valley, CA 95066
(408) 438-3100

DISC Architect
TMS, Inc.
110 West 3rd Street
P.O. Box 1358
Stillwater, OK 74076
(405) 377-0880

KAWare Disk Publisher
Knowledge Access International 2685
Marine Way
Suite 1305
Mountain View, CA 94043
(415) 969-0606
(800) 252-9273

Topix Spectrum System
Optical Media International
485 Alberto Way, 115
Los Gatos, CA 95032
(408) 395-4332

Local Area Networks and Wide Area Networks

Advanced Graphics Applications, Inc.
90 5th Avenue
New York, NY 10011
(212) 337-4200
(800) DISCUS-1

Artisoft Inc.
575 E River Road
Tucson, AZ 85704

CBIS, Inc.
5875 Peachtree Industrial Blvd Building
100, Unit 170
Norcross, GA 30092
(404) 446-1332

DSC Communications Corp
1000 Coit Road
Plano, TX 75075
(214) 519-3000

Network Research Corp
2380 N. Rose Avenue
Oxnard, CA 93030
(805) 485-2700

Network Software Associates
1920 L Street, NW
Suite 510
Washington, DC 20036
(202) 785-9168

Novell, Inc
6100 Wilshire Blvd 1150
Los Angeles, CA 90048
(213) 933-8393

3 COM Corporation
535 Anton Blvd 700
Costa Mesa, CA 92626
(714) 434-1112

Remote Software (for dial access to networks; software name appears before address)

Carbon Copy
MicroCom
951 East Railroad
Giddings, TX 78942
(409) 542-0091

CD-Ware
Logicraft
5775 Wayzata Blvd.
Minneapolis, MN 55416
(612) 545-7565

PC Anywhere
DMA Company
1317 Regal 523
Richardson, TX 75080

LOCAL ONLINE

Mini Computer and Mainframe I/R Software (Operating systems supported are listed under the address)

Abadas Natural
Software AG Systems Inc
11190 Sunrise Valley Drive
Reston, VA 22091
(800) 843-9534
(703) 860 5050
MVS/DOS,XA,ESA; VM, VAX/VMS,
Wang VS, OS/2, HP UNIX

BASIS
Information Dimensions Inc
655 Metro Place, South
Dublin, OH 43017
(800) 328-2648
(614) 761-8083
MVS/TSO, NOS/VE, ULTRIX,
VM/CMS,XA,SP; VMS/XA, Digital
VMS, Sun UNIX

BRS/Search
BRS Software Products
A Division of Maxwell Online
8000 Westpark Drive
McLean, VA 22102
(703) 442-3870
MVS/CICS, VAX/VMS, UNIX(all
varieties), VM/CMS, AOS/VS, NixPort,
Tandom, MS-DOS

FUL/TEXT
Fulcrum Technologies Inc
560 Rochester Street
Ottawa, ON K1S 5K2
(613) 238-1761
AOS/VS, UNIX, VMS, XENIX,
MS-DOS, PYRAMID OSX, APPLE
MAC, SUN/3, SUN/OS, IBM/AIX,
OS/2, DG, VAX/VMS, VAX/ULTRIX,
UNISYS 6000

Inquire
INFODATA Systems Inc.
5205 Leesburg Pike
Falls Church, VA 22041
(703) 578-3430

Knowledge Retrieval System (KRS)
KnowledgeSet Corp
888 Villa, Suite 500
Mountain View, CA 94041
(415) 968-9888
(800) 456-0469
DOS and UNIX

STAIRS
IBM
Old Orachard Road
Armonk, NY 10504
(914) 765-1900
MVS/CICS,DOS; VM/CMS

STATUS
CP International Inc
521 5th Ave 4, 7th Floor
New York, NY 10036
(212) 575-2225
AOS, DOS, GCOS-8, MS-DOS,
MULTICS, MVS, PRIMOS, UNIX,
VM/CMS, VS

TOPIC
Verity, Inc
1550 Plymouth Street
Mountain View, CA 94043
(415) 960-7600
MS-DOS, UNIX, VSM

PC Text Retrieval Software (includes CD-ROM Authoring Systems) (software name appears above the address)

BlueFish
Lotus Development Corp
55 Cambridge Parkway
Cambridge, MA 02142
(617) 577-8500

COMPACT-SEARCH
Digital Library Systems Inc
5161 River Road, Bldg 6
Bethesda, MD 20816
(301) 657-2997

Folio Views
Folio Corporation
2155 N. Freedom Blvd
Suite 150
Provo, UT 84604
(801) 375-3700
(800) 543-6546

HyperIndexer
Knowledgeset Corporation
888 Villa Street
Suite 500
Mountain View, CA 94041
(800) 456-0469
(415) 968-9888

INFORMIX-SQL
Informix Software, Inc
4100 Bohannon Drive
Menlo Park, CA 94025
(415) 926-6300

INNERVIEW
TMS, Inc.
110 W 3rd Street
P.O. Box 1358
Stillwater, OF 74076
(405) 377-0880

KAware2
Knowledge Access International 2685
Marine Way
Suite 1305
Mountain View, CA 94043
(415) 969-0606
(800) 252-9273

LaserRetrieve
Hewlett-Packard
19310 Pruneridge Avenue
Cuppertino, CA 94014
(800) 538-8787

LASERTEX
American Helix Technology Corporation
1857 Colonial Village Lane
Lancaster, PA 17601
(717) 392-7840
(800) 525-6575

ROMWARE
Nimbus Information Systems
P.O. Box 7305
Charlottesville, VA 22906
(800) 782-0778
(804) 985-1100

Quantum Leap
Quantum Access Inc
50 Briar Hollow W, Suite 515
Houston, TX 77027
(713) 622-3211

Query Plus, Full Text Manager, Image
Manager
Reference Technology Inc
5700 Flatiron Pkwy
Boulder, CO 80301
(800) 562-2015
(303) 449-4157

SearchExpress
Executive Technologies Inc
2120 16th Avenue, South
Birmingham, AL 35205
(205) 933-5494

Textbank, Memory Lane
Group L Corporation
481 Carlisle Drive
Herndon, VA 22070
(703) 471-0030
(800) 672-5300

ZyIndex
ZyLab Corp
100 Lexington Drive
Buffalo Grove, IL 60089
(800) 544-6339
(312) 459-8000

Vendors--Mini Computer or Mainframe Systems

BRS OnSite
BRS Information Technologies, A
Divison of Maxwell Online
8000 West Park Drive
McLean, VA 22102
(800) 955-0906
(703) 442-0900

NOTIS Systems, Inc.
2nd Floor
1007 Church Street
Evanston, IL 60201-3622
(708) 866-0150

STANDARDS

Standards Organizations

American Association of Publishers
2005 Massachusetts Ave, NW
Washington, DC 20036
(202) 232-3335

The Association for Computing
Machinery (ACM)
11 West 42nd Street, 3rd Floor New
York, NY 10036
(212) 869-7440

National Bureau of Standards
Administration 101, Library E-106
Gaithersburg, MD 10899
(301) 975-2814

NISO
P.O. Box 1056
Bethesda, MD 20817
975-2814